Understanding the Human Mind

The Strength of Positive Thinking

Jason Browne

© Copyright 2020 - All rights reserved.

The content contained within this book may not be reproduced, duplicated or transmitted without direct written permission from the author or the publisher.

Under no circumstances will any blame or legal responsibility be held against the publisher, or author, for any damages, reparation, or monetary loss due to the information contained within this book, either directly or indirectly.

Legal Notice:

This book is copyright protected. It is only for personal use. You cannot amend, distribute, sell, use, quote or paraphrase any part, or the content within this book, without the consent of the author or publisher.

Disclaimer Notice:

Please note the information contained within this document is for educational and entertainment purposes only. All effort has been executed to present accurate, up to date, reliable, complete information. No warranties of any kind are declared or implied. Readers acknowledge that the author is not engaged in the rendering of legal, financial, medical or professional advice. The content within this book has been derived from various sources. Please consult a licensed professional before attempting any techniques outlined in this book.

By reading this document, the reader agrees that under no circumstances is the author responsible for any losses, direct or indirect, that are incurred as a result of the use of the information contained within this document, including, but not limited to, errors, omissions, or inaccuracies.

Table of Contents

INTRODUCTION 1

CHAPTER 1: YOU ARE WHAT YOU THINK - THE POWER OF POSITIVE THINKING 7

UNDERSTANDING SOCIETAL MISCONCEPTIONS.................................. 8
WHAT IS POSITIVE PSYCHOLOGY?.. 11
WHY CHOOSE POSITIVE PSYCHOLOGY? 16
CHANGING THE NEURAL PATHWAYS 19

CHAPTER 2: REWIRING THOUGHT HABITS 21

THE DELEGATION OF NEGATIVE PATTERNS 21
   Drowning in Expectations 22
   Learned Helplessness 24
   The Inner Critic 25
   Low Self-Esteem and Self-Doubt 27
   Fearful Limitations 29
THOUGHT HABITS TO ADOPT FOR POSITIVE CHANGE 31
   Acceptance 31
   Exploration 35

CHAPTER 3: BE OPTIMISTIC, STAY HOPEFUL 37

UNDERSTANDING THE MECHANICS 37
WHAT IS BALANCED OPTIMISM?... 40
LEARNED OPTIMISM 44
   Musical Roles 45
   Challenge Your Thoughts 46
   The Best Possible Self 46
AN UNMEASURABLE BENEFIT OF OPTIMISM 47

CHAPTER 4: RETHINKING YOUR BEHAVIORAL EXPERIENCES. 49

WHY THE MIND AND BODY CONNECTION MATTERS 49

- Mental Experiences: Mindfulness 50
  - *Affirmations* 52
  - *Creative Visualization* 54
  - *Meditation* 56
- Physical Experiences 59
  - *Laughter* 59
  - *Posture* 61

CHAPTER 5: INDULGING IN GRATITUDE 63

- How Gratitude Works 63
- Assessing Gratitude 67
- Practicing Gratitude 68
  - *Journaling* 68
  - *Appreciate People* 69
  - *Quick Boosters* 70
  - *A Gratitude Challenge* 70
  - *The Gratitude Jar* 71
  - *The Appreciation Rock* 71
  - *Gratitude Meditation* 71
- Kindness, Understanding, and Gratitude 74

CHAPTER 6: EXPERIENCING FLOW 77

- Introducing Flow 77
- Why It Matters 81
- The Basics 83
- Transcending Into Flow 84

CHAPTER 7: BELIEVE IN YOURSELF AND ACKNOWLEDGE YOUR POTENTIAL 89

- Purpose and Happiness 89
- Listen for a Calling 91
- Set Goals 94
- The Required Skills 98
  - *Failure Reconstruction* 98
  - *Self-Reliance* 99
  - *Self-Resilience* 100
  - *Intuition* 103
  - *Responsibility* 103

Self-Love *104*

CHAPTER 8: POSITIVE CONNECTIONS, HEALTHY RELATIONSHIPS 107

POSITIVE PSYCHOLOGY AND RELATIONSHIPS 107
BEWARE THE ROCKS 110
BUILDING DEEP CONNECTIONS 114
Healthy Problem-Solving *114*
Generosity *116*
Compassion *117*

CHAPTER 9: MOVING FORWARD AND TAKING MATTERS INTO YOUR OWN HANDS 121

FORDYCE'S FUNDAMENTALS 121
A FINAL ENCOURAGEMENT 129

CONCLUSION... 133

REFERENCES.. 137

Introduction

Tony Dungy once said: "Be positive. Your mind is more powerful than you think. What is down in the wells comes up in the bucket. Fill yourself with positive things."

The heaving toll of a bucket filled with negative thoughts, emotions, and experiences is undeniable. It affects every aspect of your life from relationships to work to general happiness. The weight is indescribable when your life isn't going according to your dreams. At some point, the bucket is overflowing, and your life isn't what it should be. You miss a promotion at work, and you don't know how to advance your career. You don't get along with your colleagues, and your job quickly becomes a strain on your life. There's no joy and excitement as you walk into your office like a drone.

Relationships aren't what you expected, either. Some days people treat you like a throwaway tissue, and other days, they can't stop checking in and asking you for favors. The time shortly comes when you realize that you're surrounded by people who don't make you happy. Your negativity spirals even further as you lose friends, and you can't understand why you've drifted apart. Why can no one appreciate or even acknowledge the effort you make? Your romantic relationships are on and off, and you're not even sure your friends are genuine. Negativity has crept into your social life, and deconstructed it.

It's difficult to understand how this happens when you try your best to abide by societal rules. How can people be disappointed and unappreciative when you've always strived to reach their expectations. The only truth about your constant pursuit of acceptance is that you're miserable. The more you spiral into misery, the more negative you become. You don't even know how these thoughts and emotions manifest, but you never expected them after believing you live by standards that should make everyone happy. That's the problem. Everyone is happy, you're the one who is not. The only people who seem to stick around are the ones who are just as negative and joyless as yourself.

You're tired of being negative because you're starting to see how it's affecting your life. Negativity and happiness can never exist in the same space. The harder you try, the more your mind tends to push negative thoughts back into the spotlight. You don't even intend to think this way, but your emotions flood through you before you can even consider a different way of thinking. No one ever said that life was easy, but damn, this isn't it. You want to increase your happiness, and the time has come to make changes now. You want to attract the right outcomes that seem so distant right now. How does anyone change a habitual way of thinking after years of conditioning?

That's where the human mind comes into play. If only you knew the powers within. If only you had an idea of what your mind is capable of. Indeed, it's also the reason why you're trapped in this consistent cycle of negativity and unhappiness. Think about it this way. What is a doctor's first response when you enter their practice? Sure, you'll explain why you're there, and how you feel, but the doctor has one mission. They need to figure out what the source of your problem is. Maybe you've had an unusual migraine for weeks, and from years of studying and practical application the doctor knows that tests are needed to find the source. It's not a guessing game. The pain can only subside if the source is found; otherwise, you'll be treating symptoms and not the cause.

This is why your pursuit of happiness and positivity has been flawed. You can rightfully blame the brain for your dilemma, but the human mind is also the source. You need to apply scientific and proven methods to change your outlook, which will change your direction and level of satisfaction. Indeed, the human mind can be toxically negative to impact your life and fulfillment, but this conditioning has been programmed over years. It comes down to the networks within the brain, and which networks communicate with each other more often. The human mind can't be chastised for its choices, either. Its primal directive is to protect you at any cost. It's the center that must prevent any harm from overcoming you.

The human mind's primary directive causes negativity on a pandemic level, so don't feel like your life is the only one being sabotaged by it. Understandably, people are more prone to live negative and unhappy lives because the human mind always prefers to think protectively. It gets worse if you consider what our minds are fed daily. Shockingly, 90% of all media news is negative, sensationalism makes up 95% of news media, and there was a 35% increase in exaggerated news in 2019 (Djordjevic, 2020). These figures are astounding when you consider that 10% of Americans browse quick news feeds every hour, and it's more frightening because people are 49% more likely to be attracted by negative news. This proves two key factors: the human mind is biased, and so are the stories we tell and share.

The only way to change this beautiful complexity to think in new ways is to use evidence from experts. The human mind can be changed, and it can be done so with positive psychology. Traditional psychology has mainly focused on the disease model of the mind, but there isn't a connection between diseases and negative thinking; it starts elsewhere. The mind is conditioned through life experience to establish specific pathways between various regions, and this makes it easier to think that way. There's no disease involved. Indeed, chemicals in the brain can be offset by certain habits, making it harder to achieve new thoughts, but positive psychology focuses on models proven to change these pathways.

I've always been deeply fascinated by the human mind. My research over the years has helped me uncover secrets to unlocking every positive region while laying the pathways we need to live a happy life with moments we cherish, however small they might be. I rely heavily on neuroscience and psychology to guarantee results, and I practice these methods myself. The psychology models introduced by positive psychology have given me the key to the answer of whether my life is wholeheartedly worth living. Indeed, happiness is misunderstood, and my research has shown me how. This book is driven by passion, and I even found myself completely lost in the moment while writing it. You'll understand why this is important in chapter six.

You'll learn about positive psychology and the models that enhance your life from every aspect. You'll know what role society plays, and how you can use this knowledge to rewire the pathways in your brain. Some theories prove that helplessness and negative emotions are learned through years of conditioning, but this helps you to practice methods to change the way your brain fires. You'll know how to deal with the inner critics, and how your mental inhibitions have held you back. Two thought habits already lay the foundation for new thinking.

Optimism is also a misunderstood concept because people call you Pollyanna when you skip through life with a smile and bounce in your step. Optimism and positivity aren't the same things entirely, and you'll learn how to understand balanced optimism so that it leads to your desired mindset. The exercises are so simple, and the ultimate benefit can't be matched. Turning the mind positive is one step, but you'll also connect the mind and body to behave positively, too. Positive behavior is a reflection of your inner happiness, allowing you to share your new life with the people who matter. You'll learn about the one trait that pushes your positive journey ahead, and you'll have many ways of practicing it.

Most importantly, there's a well-known secret to living a happy, positive, and fulfilling life—having a purpose. Even positive psychology teaches you that having a purpose in life is the key to happiness. It's essential to find your calling and know how to answer it. The advantages of a meaningful life are boundless in mental, emotional, and physical well-being. Most often, people are too afraid to take the first step toward their purpose, but you'll learn how to remove this fear. It's merely an obstacle, which is another one of life's displeasures you'll manage well. Planning your life with the help of experts and proven advice is how you take that first step, and you'll adopt the six skills needed for it to work.

The life you dreamed about, the positivity you wish to possess, and everything you hoped for are within this book. It comes in a practical form that allows you to make the changes you need without a struggle. The only encouragement now is to take the first step into chapter one.

Chapter 1:

You Are What You Think - The Power of Positive Thinking

At this point in your life, especially if you're reading this book, you're probably feeling a hint of dissatisfaction and unhappiness with how your life has gone. It's time to reflect on your life and how society has formed your definition of what happiness must look like. Once you understand the falsities surrounding a life worth living, you can learn about positive psychology (PP) and its main components before tackling the various areas of your life. Change is not only possible; it's inevitable when you use the power of the mind. There's nothing far-fetched about what you're about to achieve.

Understanding Societal Misconceptions

Ask yourself the key question before continuing. Are you genuinely happy with your life's direction right now? If you're reading this, your answer is most likely 'no' or "not quite." Take a moment of pause to reflect on what's been happening, and recognize where and how your life started going downhill. Life deserves to move in an alternate direction, right? The first important reminder is that it's not your fault. Modern society is structured in a way that promotes happiness as a commodity and forgets all about the necessity of it. The hierarchical society, capitalism, and patriarchy have made it near impossible to see happiness for what it is. Our society has set unrealistic ground rules that can't be met unless you're one of the creators.

Very few people are capable of finding happiness in this warped society. If you don't look like a supermodel in a magazine, own a beach house, or wear enough Gucci to make a grown man cry, then you aren't happy enough. Society expects you to be wealthy, successful, and conform in every way. You have to look like this, think like that, and behave the way everyone expects you to. You'll never be good enough if you aren't influential. You start believing that you must be doing something wrong, and there's nothing you can do that's enough to impress the masses. In a nutshell, you're a nobody if you don't conform to impossible standards, and that idea can make you endlessly miserable.

This misconception needs to change because you can't stay oblivious to the negative influence that's gradually destroying you. Unfortunately, we end up going into a never-ending cycle of negativity, and worse is that our brains are biologically wired to be negative, making the cycle more destructive. We can blame evolution for this one. Millenia earlier, our ancestors had to consider the dangers in the world to survive daily. They had to hunt to eat, and they had to consider the predators that were higher on the food chain, or they wouldn't eat. The human brain has been programmed to scan potential threats to survive because our first and foremost instinct is to preserve our lives.

Only the strong survived ancient times, and sadly, their genes were passed through generations, leading to a modern society that has ill-gotten misconceptions of what truly matters in life. Have you ever wondered why a first impression is so powerful, especially when it's negative? Don't you wonder why you'll continue to think about the coffee you spilled on your white shirt before going into a meeting, but conveniently you will forget details of the meeting? This is called negativity bias in psychology, and it's the primal part of the brain that focuses on threats more than positive experiences (Cherry & Swaim, 2019). It's an evolution that didn't go too well.

The human brain is biologically predisposed to focus on negative events, insults, and trauma more than positive experiences, pleasures, and compliments. The brain has billions of neurons, and between them are trillions of synapses, with which one neuron communicates with another one with neurotransmitters. Your negativity bias is born in infancy. It exists from as early as three-months-old, explaining why babies cry when they feel uncomfortable. As long as the survival instinct is present, the brain will latch on to the defense mode that protects us, and society doesn't help if they continue to make us believe that reality is so and so.

The stronger these synapses become from consistent negative communication, the deeper the beliefs embed themselves in your mind. It's a habit to pursue money because your core belief installed by society has told you that you must be wealthy to be happy. Your motivation is also stumped because the brain will rather motivate you to complete a task that prevents the loss of something, such as wealth, instead of motivating you to pursue the gain of something new, which might be authentic happiness. It's time for you to make the distinction because you can't be happy unless you understand what's happening, recognize where you are now, and start making subtle changes to your thought and belief systems because these systems influence your behavior.

Take one more reflective moment, and ask yourself the fundamental questions that help you to recognize societal misconceptions in the definition of happiness.

What is your main focus right now?

How does your main focus not benefit your well-being?

Are there things in your life that you're happy and satisfied with?

Is your happiness based on societal standards, or do these things genuinely make you happy?

Take some time to think about one thing that makes you happy, and pay attention to the changes you experience while you focus on it. *Does it make you feel lighter, calmer, or do you breathe easier?*

This little reflection experiment helps you to understand how positive thinking can have instantaneous benefits on your well-being. Living by societal rules can only make you miserable because you'll never meet their standards, even though your second instinct is to fit into the crowd. Social needs are the second instinct we inherited from the earliest humans. The fear of not meeting society's standards is a direct threat to our survival instinct because rejection from society sets alarms off in the brain. Psychology can help you navigate away from this societal misconception without breaking the connections you need in your life.

What is Positive Psychology?

PP is the opposite of the rudimentary and traditional forms of psychology, and it was Psychologist Martin Seligman who blew the top off this raving concept that's led to numerous studies and theories (Ackerman, 2019). Seligman was unhappy with the traditional approach of psychology because it focused on the negative, traumatic, depressive, and suffering side of humankind. Ironically, even traditional psychology has a negative bias. Seligman wanted to focus on the well-being of patients instead of treating negative emotions, including subjective well-being, which already cuts around the societal rules.

His work with depression patients in the 1960s led to one of his many great achievements. Seligman proved that people were capable of learned helplessness, and his research focused on helping patients learn optimism, virtues, and varied perspectives instead, which helped them adopt authentic happiness because it was subjective. Bringing someone out of depression can be achieved by making them forget about the objective happiness that society expects and turn their happiness into a subjective pursuit while respecting the social aspect. Seligman helped to redirect psychology to promote life-improvement instead of life-depletion.

Positive psychology focuses on a different route. Happiness is the ultimate cause of a life worth living, and in turn, a good life makes people subjectively happy. Even money doesn't bring good returns on happiness because you can't buy it. You might be able to buy some happiness by helping other people reach their good life, but the money just becomes stagnant after you have what you need. PP focuses on authentic happiness instead. Eudaimonia is the definition of authentic happiness, which is quite different from hedonism. Hedonism is when you find temporary happiness in the endless pursuit of pleasure, the absence of distress, and the need for everything to be perfectly enjoyable.

So, what happens when life isn't enjoyable? Hedonism can never be realistic. It's the type that society sets, and it can't be reached because it mainly belongs to external factors. Society says that you must be wealthy to be happy, so this is their standard. Do you think a wealthy person with no children, family, and time to enjoy life is truly happy? What about the working-class man who has a family at home, everything his children need, and a loving wife? Is he supposed to be less satisfied with his life if he has all he needs? Hedonic happiness also expects that you can't experience any setbacks because this doesn't bring a steady stream of pleasures.

Positive psychology focuses on eudaimonia, which translates to authenticity, growth, meaning, excellence, flourishing, and well-being. It's an intrinsic type of happiness that focuses on the journey and not just the outcome. Well-being isn't an outcome anyway. It's a journey between here and there. Translating the word 'eudaimonia' etymologically will also give you a deeper meaning. The 'eu' means good or well, and the 'daimon' stands for spirit. Positive psychology might teach you to focus on intrinsic well-being, but it also adopts the virtues required to be a good spirit or person, which means that your pursuit of success and happiness will still include meaningful connections to other people.

Eudaimonia is a deeper kind of happiness that we require to find meaning in our lives. It's a form of well-being that can't be met by hedonic pursuits of temporary pleasures. Indeed, external factors can still influence your life, but that's where your learned mastery of virtues will see you through. Perhaps, your virtue is courage, which is between cowardice and recklessness. Being courageous allows you to learn from making mistakes instead of cowering away from them or being reckless enough to allow external factors to deter your journey. Eudaimonia is also the type of happiness that allows you to measure your progress in a good life because you aren't focused on the outcome alone.

You'll learn who you really are, develop unique potentials, and use those potentials to reach your ultimate life goals. The heart also matters far more than your head in PP, meaning that compassion and empathy are as important as your critical thoughts. Your ultimate pursuit in life will become that of having a good life where your intrinsic happiness is a priority, you still cherish the connection to other people, you believe in yourself, and you have a sense of control. The greatest news is that "the good life" can also be taught. Positive psychology focuses on experiences beyond happiness, such as love and inspiration. It also teaches you how to master strengths that promote the good life, including resilience, compassion, and gratitude.

Moreover, this form of psychology elevates your good life in such a way that it benefits, encourages, and inspires people around you so that everyone in your sphere can lead a better life. You gain a new perspective that helps you thrive, and it can help your community do the same. Seligman introduced a model that would change the world of psychology. The PERMA model was developed to understand genuine happiness.

PERMA is an acronym devised by Seligman to define what is required in a good life to guarantee well-being, happiness, and success. Each factor can't create happiness on its own, but together, they create a life worth living.

- The 'P' is for positive emotions, meaning you need to experience positive emotions by enjoying yourself in the moment.
- The 'E' stands for engagement, and you must engage deeply in an experience so that you get lost in the moment. You must become absorbed by tasks you're good at and enjoy.
- The 'R' is for positive relationships, and you must be the social creature that makes up for the second instinct. We all desire a meaningful connection to someone else, or we won't genuinely flourish.
- 'M' for meaning because no person can be happy without a purpose. You must find meaning in your life, and this might be a dedication to a cause or knowing that we're simply a cog in the machine that drives a bigger purpose.
- The 'A' is for accomplishment or achievement, and requires you to grow and improve yourself, including your strengths.

Why Choose Positive Psychology?

The benefits of practicing PP are endless, and many of them have been confirmed through science (Ackerman, 2019). You can see all the improvements in your life once you shift your perspective of the potential for happiness in your daily life. Reaching for a good life instead of focusing on societal values helps you to lead a happier life. You'll also learn to master gratitude so that you can rightfully recognize all the moments you have to be grateful for. Positive emotions can enhance your work performance, leading to greater possibilities. You can even encourage the workplace to become happier when the societal definitions of happiness are gone and replaced with small, genuine boosts of joy.

Moreover, positivity is contagious in the workplace. Apply this benefit at home and you'll have happier kids, partners, and friendships. Kindness and compassion toward other people don't only boost your happiness; it also makes other people more receptive of you, which is rather the opposite of what society tries to make you believe. PP is used in relationships to promote balance, genuine love, and lasting connections. Upholding a positive relationship is good for everyone, and another way of understanding the benefits of PP is that it aims to help individuals and communities thrive simultaneously.

Your positive mood could inspire those around you to seek the same intrinsic rewards that you experience in an elevated existence. Everyone inspires the next person, and there's no envy, sabotage, or unhealthy exchange involved. Not using positive psychology in relationships can lead to serious consequences for everyone involved. Without seeking a mutually beneficial good life, one or both partners can suffer from depression, anxiety, insecurities, commitment problems, trust issues, communication hassles, and avoidance of future relationships. We need relationships to be happy in this life, so you must handle your life with a positive attitude.

You can benefit from practicing PP as it builds up freedom, self-confidence, productivity, focus, and the overall desire to lead a healthy, balanced life. There are even differences in the way your brain communicates when you think positively or negatively. The brain is plastic (bear with me); this is both good and bad. The synapses and networks within the brain can change to create patterns, which we call habits (Whitaker, 2018). The brain fires communications between the synapses with every thought that crosses your mind. It will release neurotransmitters like cortisol when you feel anxious. However, happy thoughts release serotonin, which suppresses the stress hormone, regulates your moods, and creates a feeling of well-being.

Dopamine is another optimistic neurotransmitter, which activates the brain's reward and pleasure centers. Positive thoughts and feelings can activate the higher processing in your prefrontal cortex. Your focus peaks, you become more creative, and your cognitive flexibility enhances when the prefrontal cortex is functioning at full steam ahead. Your attention span increases, and your focus shifts to 'us' instead of 'me,' which is essential for a good life that involves community inspiration and happiness. The prefrontal cortex experiences growth in the number of synapses between neurons when you remain positive. This part of your brain is key to many other regions in the brain and body.

It's the first stop for conscious thoughts, and it can activate various communications, including the emotional and logical parts of the brain. You can control the emotions from the limbic system deeper in the brain by consciously using the prefrontal cortex. It's also the only place where metacognition occurs, the ability to be aware of your own thoughts. Negative thinking can cause metabolic energy to be redirected away from the prefrontal cortex, making it less possible for the brain to perform at a higher function. For example, being stressed and thinking the worst can switch the brain's creativity and ability to process new information. Stress or negative thoughts can also slow down the cerebellum, which is responsible for balance, coordination, and the pace of thoughts.

This also helps you understand the negativity bias on a neurological level because the synapses will keep growing to reinforce this negative behavior, and it can be influenced by the simplest of things. Sometimes, it isn't even the criticism from someone that hurts us; it's simply the tone of their voice that makes us feel questionable. Negative thoughts can hinder your decision-making, and disrupt your impulse controls in the left temporal lobe. Luckily you can use neuroplasticity to enhance your problem-solving, creativity, productivity, and focus with a positive outlook.

Changing the Neural Pathways

Repetition is your best friend when creating new pathways in the brain. Generally, it takes about 10,000 repetitions to install new pathways, or three to six months of practicing new habits does the trick for most (Hani, 2017). Repeating a positive mindset will encourage the brain to store this new information as the chosen habit, and your behavior and thought patterns will become automatic. Prompting the brain to create new pathways to various brain regions will further promote new habits. The only way you can truly trick the brain into creating new pathways to emotional centers, coordination glands, and the speed of thought is to use your five senses like a glue that strengthens the experiences so that they can be stored in long-term memory.

The senses require multiple centers in the brain to activate, and this designs the network you desire between the prefrontal cortex and other regions. The process will be tough, but don't let it dishearten you. Commit yourself to positive thinking, and watch how your habits change, which in turn, changes your quality of life when you experience positive benefits. The goal is to connect as many senses as you can to every experience you want to repeat. This is also part of the PERMA model, which encourages you to engage fully in the experience. Don't just set a goal. Experience the dream with items you can smell, touch, feel, see, and taste to make it stick in your mind. Also, never settle for just the dream.

Your behaviors and the sensory experience you enjoy while acting them out will glue the memory to your synapses. A simple understanding of this is to recall any happy memory where you were maybe enjoying a road trip. You see amazing sights on this trip, and you even say out loud how beautiful the mountain range is, but you don't commit to engaging in the experience. You'll forget all about the beauty in a matter of days or hours. However, if you pull over and experience the beauty with your senses for 30 seconds, then you'll remember what you saw. Focus on the emotions of how this beauty makes you feel, too.

Positive emotional and sensory experiences are the best ways to absorb the memory, leaving it in your thought bucket until you need it. You're more likely to remember certain behaviors and repeat them if they were associated with positive emotions. Human evolution might not be on your side, and neither are the biological processes that keep certain patterns in the brain, but you can use the revolution of positive psychology and positive thinking to rewire your brain for ultimate success, happiness, and better relationships.

Chapter 2:

Rewiring Thought Habits

Negative thoughts and emotions are embedded deeply in your psychology as a flawed part of your evolution, but that doesn't mean that you can't transform them into more productive ones. Negative emotions aren't entirely bad per se, but being overwhelmed by them is a recipe for a miserable life. The next step in your journey is to rethink the negative habits and how to use the correct tools to deal with them.

The Delegation of Negative Patterns

Start rewiring your brain by being self-aware of paying attention to your thoughts. It will feel alien or awkward to think differently at first. However, the temporary awkwardness around unfamiliar thoughts is worth it in the end. Consider a few questions before moving ahead.

How high are your expectations of other people and yourself?

Do you succumb to feelings of helplessness when change is certain?

Are you highly critical of yourself?

Do you doubt yourself or your capabilities?

Do you battle against low self-esteem?

Do you incessantly fear changes?

Finally, ask yourself why you answered these questions the way you did. Certain thought habits stop you from being optimistic, and they can wreak havoc on your mental well-being.

Drowning in Expectations

Having unrealistic expectations can lead to low self-esteem, depression, chronic stress, perfectionism, the fear of failure, the fear of change, and perfectionism. You'll drown in negativity, and have no faith in your abilities. It's not only your expectations, either. The standards set by society and those you love can also impact your life. The expectations set by others guide the standards you hold over yourself. The truth is that no one can meet unrealistic expectations, nor you or a friend. You might feel overly critical about an upcoming project, feel resentment toward the people you think are expecting you to be better, or you might feel guilty because you failed. High expectations can lead to a life of endless negativity cycles because failure is a possibility, but the fear of it can cripple you.

You'll miss opportunities that often disguise themselves in setbacks because you're afraid of letting people down. Even worse, you're afraid of letting yourself down. Additionally, you'll wallow in a blackhole of criticism because you can only blame yourself for missing your expectations. If you fear failure, obsess over the details, or find yourself smacking your forehead when you make a mistake, you're most likely being a little unrealistic in your standards, or you care too much about other people's expectations. It's time to let go of these expectations. Unrealistic standards are another byproduct of our beliefs if parents expected the best from us with every exam, or our employers expect nothing less than a wow.

Believe it or not, expectations aren't all bad. They are the standards we set to achieve our goals, and we can set realistic expectations of outcomes, or at least, something similar. That's the biggest problem with expectations. We have an exact idea of an outcome, but remember that being positive and happy means that you must enjoy the journey, too. The outcome hardly ever works as you want it to, so stop expecting perfection. Always expect the best because it's the only way you'll achieve the greatest result, but don't be hard on yourself if it differs slightly. Be flexible, and commit to a certain outcome, but be happy with something similar.

Lower your daily expectations of yourself and the people around you if they're unrealistic. Everyone will make a mistake at some point, so lower expectations prevent too many perceived errors. Moreover, stop expecting the worst from yourself and others. No one can stay on a pedestal, and you'll only hurt your relationships if you do this. Before setting any standard in your life, ask yourself:

Is this what I genuinely want and need?

Will this expectation serve me?

Could it hold me back?

What would I lose if I let go of this expectation?

What would I gain if I let go of it?

Learned Helplessness

Learned helplessness is vastly tied to depression and negative emotions. People who continually face seemingly uncontrollable or negative situations, try to change it, fail to do so, and quit trying altogether are suffering from learned helplessness. Often, they can change it if they try with the right expectations, but they don't because mistakes make them cringe. Take an alcoholic, for example. They know that their habit is harmful, and they try to quit but end up drinking again, so they quit trying to stop their habit. This is learned helplessness because they have the power to stop their habit just as a pessimist can change their outlook on life. Have you ever been depressed?

You feel like there's no end to the battle when you're depressed, even though there's always an end to every story. Learned helplessness also lowers your self-esteem, motivation, and determination. The three greatest traits to learn to combat helplessness are self-compassion, resilience, and self-worth, which are essential in a good life, and optimism. Learned optimism is the most powerful combatant for learned helplessness, which we'll focus on later. Becoming a positive thinker empowers you again, taking back what learned helplessness has taken away from you. Optimism and happiness are impossible without empowerment. Only you can make the necessary changes, and this knowledge alone is empowering.

The Inner Critic

Another negative habit is the inner critic. How harsh is your inner critic if you had to rate it on a scale from one to ten? The inner critic can be a reflection of unrealistic standards, but it wears many faces. You get the inadequate critic that criticizes mistakes, the self-hate critic that creates unhealthy animosity toward yourself, and the constructive inner critic. Depending on which type you hear, a negative mindset is only one consequence. You can also suffer from depression, anxiety, and self-sabotage (Parker, 2020). Self-sabotage is an intense form of pessimism that indulges you in self-defeating behaviors because you can't meet unrealistic expectations.

It's a dangerous path, and there's no way you can find happiness or success while the self-hate critic is convincing you to do the unthinkable. It can be as extreme as suicidal thoughts or addictive behaviors like alcoholism, drug addiction, and eating disorders. The only critic that must be active is the constructive one, which helps you to see greater detail when pursuing a goal. Any other critic needs to be faced, silenced, or defeated for you to overcome the chronic pessimism that prevents you from enjoying a good life. Becoming aware of the inner voice is the first step.

Self-criticism came from somewhere. It serves a purpose in our lives, but who installed it? Pay attention to your inner dialogue when you face a problem. Just remember to listen compassionately because being too harsh will only make you criticize your inner critic, and this begins a new cycle of self-criticism. Adopt the art of diffusion by acknowledging the inner critic, but know that it doesn't always speak the truth. It's only an opinion, albeit a self-view. Change the way you face the critic by realizing that what they say is merely an idea. There isn't always evidence to prove what they're saying. This slowly takes power away from the inner critic when truths become ideas.

If you find it hard to recognize thoughts as ideas, then adopt the self-distancing strategy taught by cognitive-behavioral therapy (Pincott, 2019). Step out of your mind and talk to your inner critic from a third-person perspective. Replace the word 'I' with he, she, or your name while you respond. It might say that you're not good enough to apply for the promotion at work. Respond to this inner voice by saying: "So, you think that she isn't good enough, but what about her project that won an award last year?" Stepping into a distanced state also allows you to speak to your inner critic as though it's a friend. It isn't always an enemy, so face and silence it by treating it compassionately like a friend.

Defeating the negative inner critic is also achieved over time. Challenge it when it gets too loud. Find evidence that refutes the inner criticism before it worsens. Step back into your third-person perspective and present your evidence. Do this in front of the mirror. The inner critic is the district attorney, and you are the defense attorney. The previous example already gives you an idea. She won an award for a presentation, so why would she not be eligible for the promotion? Allow the inner critic to make its case, and then you must defend your 'friend.' What needs to be considered if you were talking to a good friend who doubts herself right now?

Another method for gradually defeating an inner critic is to remove labels. The inner critic calls you stupid, poor, and unattractive, so counter its argument by letting it know that these 'labels' are only ideas again. Tell it: "You think that she's unattractive. That's your opinion and not mine." Labels generalize people. For example, calling someone stupid for making one mistake is generalizing them as non-intelligent. Is anyone judged solely by one mistake or action? Remove the labels from your inner critic, and you'll also slowly defeat it.

Low Self-Esteem and Self-Doubt

Comparing yourself to society and its standards is a recipe for low self-esteem and doubt. There are obvious signs of low self-esteem and self-doubt, but there are also less obvious signs. Being sensitive to criticism, social awkwardness, and hostility or defensiveness indicates low self-esteem, and so can obsession over problems and unexplained physical symptoms, such as fatigue and insomnia. Being afraid to try something new, doubting yourself, and having no trust in yourself are also signs. Overthinking, being afraid of changes, and frequent emotional problems also indicate low self-esteem.

One sign that many people ignore is when we're hard on ourselves, always criticizing ourselves, yet, we're lenient to other people. Overworking, overachieving, or underachieving are subtle signs of low self-esteem. The causes of low self-esteem range between expectations, societal standards, disapproving authority figures, and uninvolved caregivers during childhood. Other childhood causes include conflicting authority figures, being bullied without support by your parents, and being bullied with over-supportive or uninvolved parents according to psychologist Suzanne Lachmann (Lachmann, 2013).

Being academically challenged in childhood without getting support from parents is another common cause of self-doubt. Physical, sexual, or emotional trauma also ignites low self-esteem. The media, society, our parents, other authority figures, and even our peers have set our self-beliefs, good or not, and they determine how confident we are in ourselves. This is merely about understanding, and it doesn't mean that you must feel sorry for or blame yourself. Boosting your self-esteem means that you must get to know your authentic self, what you stand for, and what you truly desire. Then, you must take strides toward the desires you want so that you can build confidence with each step.

Surround yourself with positivity and the right kind of people, and stop comparing yourself to unique individuals because you're also uniquely talented and skilled. Acknowledge what needs to change in your life, and repeat positive affirmations to install this new perspective that you're adopting. Surely, the first change you want is to be positive and happy. Taking care of yourself is another foundation of high self-esteem and zero self-doubts. Become self-compassionate, and give yourself a further boost by giving back to society. You aren't here to meet their standards. You're here to set new standards that benefit everyone because positive living means that you must consider changes that benefit the whole community in your life.

You must accept yourself for who you are, try new things, and learn to live in the present moment. Also, spread your wings to strengthen your virtues. Everyone is good at something. Maybe you just haven't found your strength yet.

Fearful Limitations

Fear is an emotion we are all familiar with. It drives our decisions and prevents us from taking chances. Fear can limit your full potential. You won't be able to gain the most of what this book offers unless you learn to overcome your fears. Change is the one thing that strikes fear in everyone. The fear of the unknown is a heavy burden. Change is the only constant in life, and you'll be applying many changes in this book, so fearing it will stop your journey. Fear stands in the way of you making positive changes in your life, and it prevents you from eliminating destructive behaviors that prevent the changes. You won't take risks, pursue goals, or adopt a growth mindset.

Fear is merely a perception that uncertainty is fraught with potential failures. However, do you consider that uncertainty might lead to great potential? Fear only holds you back, and you must become aware of how it prevents you from reaching your fullest potential to overcome it. Fear makes us only see the negative side of possibilities. You're so consumed by the possibility of striking out when you ask a woman on a date that you decide to avoid her instead. This woman could've helped you to reach a good life, being the positive soul she is, but you decided to give up instead.

How often do you see only the negative side of opportunities? Another sign of mismanaged fear is that you can't think things through because the fear paralyzes you. You can't try new things, or you feel constricted in your societal lifestyle, not being able to say what's on your mind. Maybe fear makes you avoid any instinctual decisions, and sometimes, the best decisions come from our gut instincts. The most crippling sign of fear is when you can't make decisions. You find yourself procrastinating because making a decision is scary enough. The good news is that fear isn't all that bad if you manage it.

It heightens your alertness, and it prevents you from succumbing to disaster when your brain switches to the fight or flight response that stops you from running a red light. Your senses and awareness are temporarily elevated so that your body is prepared for a threat. You must possess a healthy amount of fear if you want to reach your fullest potential, but you cannot allow it to overwhelm you. Being transparent with yourself is frightening, but think of fear as an invitation to explore the unknown. Space would still be a mystery if fear of it wasn't conquered. Fear invites you to learn new things about yourself, your skills, and your virtues. Embrace it, and let it be an advantage instead of a handicap.

Thought Habits to Adopt for Positive Change

You've discovered the habits that restrict you, but you can adopt new habits that help you manage the negative ones and live a good life. Acceptance and exploration are the two most valuable habits you'll gain at the beginning of this journey.

Acceptance

The word itself is hard to swallow, but acceptance is the first positive habit you need. Learn to accept what you have no control over and what has already happened. There will always be something you can't change, so refusing to accept it internalizes negative feelings. Acceptance can't always be forced, but accepting that change is inevitable helps you to find acceptance of the small methods you use to pursue it. Let's say that you don't accept losing your job. The first question that pops into your mind is "why me?" You worked for this company for 20 years, and now they retrenched you as part of a large cutdown.

You see it as a personal failure. Refusing to accept the truth makes you wear delusional blinders. It must be something you did wrong. You can't accept the fact that ten other people lost their jobs, and you internalize the blame. Not being able to accept things is how you internalize negative self-doubt, criticism, fear, anger, and a feeling of lost control. The only truth is that you can't control everything in this world. Maybe you can't accept yourself after gaining weight during quarantine.. How does the refusal to accept the current situation change the outcome?

You need to accept yourself as you are, curves and all because this is the only way to accept that you need to change the situation. Acceptance can help you remove the barriers that prevent change. The past is gone and unchangeable, but you can change what you do next. Our refusal to accept changes is sometimes based on those societal expectations. So, what if your skin is flawed? Who cares if you're short? You must accept the person who stands in front of the mirror, or you won't be able to reach your fullest potential. Your inner critic will only amplify its attack.

The importance of acceptance lies internally. Learning to accept things you can't control brings positive changes to your life. You'll have more faith in yourself because you won't stand in your own way anymore. Your mind will think logically again once the internalized stress is gone. You'll find your happiness, giving you more strength to move forward. You might regret not accepting the changes sooner, but you must hush the inner critic again. You'll gain well-deserved pride, integrity, and motivation once you know that you're only human like everyone else. This newfound motivation can even make you quit unhealthy habits because change is but a word now that you know it's inevitable.

According to Therapist Joseph Wilner, you'll improve your mental and physical well-being, gain a positive attitude, and suffer from less stress (Wilner, 2013). You'll have far more energy to change the possibilities that you can, and your resilience toward future changes will increase. You'll also adopt a compassionate perspective, higher gratitude, and self-appreciation, making your self-esteem rise to new levels. Embracing acceptance is only possible when you let go of the past and learn to cope with failure, especially when you have no control over it. Striving for meaningful goals that you can accept and control also helps. Accept that you can't always be in control.

Being a control freak only limits the opportunities you should embrace to lead a happier life. Control freaks rarely know that they're being controlling, so recognize the signs of being one. Ask yourself a few questions to determine your behavior.

- Do you often try to change things about someone else to make them suit your ideas better?
- Do you micromanage people to do things your way?
- Are you overly judgmental of other people's decisions?

- Are your intentions shy of being mutually beneficial when you offer someone constructive criticism?
- Do you change your authentic-self to receive acceptance from other people?
- Do you try to influence someone's decisions by only presenting the worst-case scenarios?
- Do you find it hard to not know everything? Do you feel the need to endlessly explain your actions?

Answering yes to any of these questions indicates controlling behavior. You're only responsible for yourself and your behaviors, so you can't micromanage people. You must be vulnerable with people to see their perspective without compromising your values. Challenge your thoughts by querying whether your response to a change is reasonable. Make sure that you understand all factors that relate to the change, even if you must learn something new. Take small steps to acceptance by starting with accepting yourself. Accept that you might be a control freak, but don't condemn yourself for it.

Acknowledging the controlling behavior is enough to accept that change is needed, and if your controlling behavior leans toward perfectionism, you can reframe your idea of rest. Rest is an essential element that every human needs, and reframing it as "recovery time" is a bypass around the urge to be in control. Accept that you need recovery time to be your most productive version again.

Learning to accept thoughts for what they are—opinions. Are these thoughts helpful, true, habitual, or accepting? Ask yourself one of a few questions that helps you to accept the truth.

What is my truth in reality?

How do I want to feel when I accept a change, and how can I make it happen?

What is the best outcome of accepting a past mistake?

Would I change my authentic-self if I had to accept this thought or outcome?

Keep chipping away at unhelpful thoughts until you find the truth that acceptance isn't as hard as it seems at first. It doesn't change who you are.

Exploration

The second habit to adopt is the exploration of a vast range of positive emotions, part of which will help you navigate away from the negative emotions in this chapter. Don't forget to also enjoy pleasurable experiences, but start exploring positive emotions consciously. Gratitude is one of the emotions you must adopt, but we'll focus on it in another chapter. Joy is a comfortable and gentle form of happiness, which can be attained by doing things you love. Joy is personal to you, but it brings short bursts of happiness that help to keep your mind positive. Serenity can bring calmness to your wildly negative mind and interest helps you to move closer to your ambitions.

Hope is the anticipation of happiness, and a positive pride void of arrogance is a great accomplishment. Amusement is when you use humor to increase your subjective happiness, and inspiration is a strong motivational force to add. Awe brings intrinsic bliss, and love is a powerful emotion that brings your good life to fruition. Altruism helps you feel grateful when you help other people, and satisfaction is the intimate pleasure you feel when you achieve goals. Relief is another positive emotion that makes you recognize that the fearful, imagined outcome wasn't as bad as you thought.

Working through your negative and positive emotions to negotiate a better outcome in your life ultimately leads to a good life.

Chapter 3:

Be Optimistic, Stay Hopeful

This chapter teaches you about a crucial aspect of positive psychology—optimism. You can't adopt a positive outlook on life without optimism. Optimism has effectively proven to show a wide range of positive effects on people. You'll learn to have something to look forward to, and the weight of setbacks will decrease substantially. A realistic dose of optimism can take you a long way on your journey to a good life.

Understanding the Mechanics

It helps to know what pessimism is first. There are three mechanics of pessimism. Indeed, it's evolutionary, but the brain also has a habitual way of processing attention and information. It's a matter of selective attention. Your focus determines whether the glass is half full or empty. Any amount of water should be a positive environmental cue if you're thirsty, but do you pay attention to the presence or absence of water?

Someone with a positive outlook will filter and disregard the information that there's a shared absence and presence in the glass. Their selective attention only focuses on the presence.

The second mechanic of pessimism is your locus of control. Every brain has a control mechanism for processing information, and this locus is intricately connected to your confidence or self-competency. Anyone with enough confidence to control the realistic environment will confidently see the presence of water in the glass. They'll also realize that they can always fill the glass. A healthy internal locus of control is tied to optimism because you feel like you have realistic control over the environment. However, an external locus of control is pessimistic. Only you can control a pliable environment. You can't expect external factors to do it for you.

An external locus of control lacks self-efficacy, meaning that you feel like it's beyond your control, even if it isn't. You feel helpless to change relationships or get the best result at work because the environment is unrealistically not in your favor. There's undoubtedly an overlap between self-efficacy and luck, but having realistic expectations and competence in your abilities helps you to distinguish luck from ability. The third mechanic of pessimism is your explanatory style. A pessimist globalizes any internal, albeit temporary failures. For example, your relationship failed, so you must be the most unlovable person on earth.

One failed exam means that you must be the fourth member of *The Three Stooges*. One failure becomes an internal truth, whereas optimists tend to accept that external factors can also influence their success. They accept responsibility, but they know that the external environment can also make them fail. Their relationship failed because their partner wasn't who they were looking for. It doesn't make them unlovable; it simply means that they weren't compatible. Remember that optimists will have an internal locus of control, so they know that they have some control over the next outcome.

It's also crucial to know that optimism and positive thinking aren't quite the same things. Optimism is important to rewire your mind with positive thoughts, but there are three significant differences between them. Optimism is a personality trait, whereas positive thinking is a decision. It doesn't mean that you can't learn optimism, but it requires practice. Highly optimistic people can also have blind spots where the brain automatically filters out negative feed, but positive thinking is when you choose to see the positive edge while still being aware of the negative part without letting it deter you. In other words, positive thinking differs vastly from wearing rose-colored glasses.

The final distinction between the two is that optimism makes assumptions about the world, and positive thinking is how you accept that you can respond realistically to external factors with internal courage. These differences mean that you can be positive enough to create your own future, but adopting optimism is essential because it's an underlying trait. Becoming optimistic comes with a note of caution though. Simply forcing yourself to be this way overnight does more harm than good. You could switch over to unrealistic views swiftly, which is just as detrimental as extreme pessimism.

Seligman never intended for people to become Pollyanna personality types who wear rose-colored glasses (Ackerman, 2019). A Pollyanna can't see negative aspects. They wear blinders to block out negativity, and this won't lead to a good life. Optimism requires a gradual learned change of mind and habits to strike the right balance.

What is Balanced Optimism?

Much like learned helplessness, optimism is a trait we can learn. Pessimists see challenges in every opportunity that arises, but optimists see opportunities hiding among the challenges. Optimism is the belief that the outcome will be acceptable or successful to some extent. Some people use optimism as their explanatory style where they try to explain what happened most positively. Optimists also don't assume that failure is permanent because they accept that external states are temporary. The causes of problems are also external and not internal, specific, and not global. Just because one failure led to a negative outcome doesn't mean that it's off the table.

Balanced optimism and wishful thinking are as distant as black and white. It's a way of looking at life as a positive person who's at least in some control of the outcome. You become less susceptible to negative emotions that only lead to depression and anxiety. The first reason why optimism is balanced in PP is that people would take unnecessary risks with their finances, health, and future if they wore rose-colored glasses. Three types of balanced optimism are good for you. Big optimism is when you realize that things are going well, and it's a great time to be alive. Small optimism is when you focus on specific daily positives, such as making it on time for work.

Tiny optimism is when you feel comfortable that you'll make it through the day, even if there are some challenges. To encounter all three types of optimism, you need to get those pathways engraved in the brain. Neuroscience teaches us the difference between optimism and pessimism (Positive Psychlopedia, 2015). The positive regions in the brain include the nucleus accumbens, which are an essential collection of neurons that connect your brain to a vast network of pleasure and reward centers. They're deeply stored near the hypothalamus in the midbrain, and they thrive on feel-good chemicals like serotonin, dopamine, and natural opioid neurotransmitters.

They offer reinforcement and motivation. This system is connected to the prefrontal cortex, depending on how engraved your positive thoughts become. The negative brain includes the emotional amygdala, which centers itself around fear and the stress response. The prefrontal cortex is the conscious thinker that must process information to determine whether we fear a situation or whether we can find some hint of pleasure in surviving the challenge. Even if you know that fear is irrational, you'll still experience its enormity if your amygdala isn't under control from the prefrontal cortex.

We all have both systems engraved into our brains, but it depends on which pathways we encourage to develop. One thing we have much control over is our explanatory style or how we explain the causes and effects of a negative situation. How do you explain negative events? Do you label yourself as unlikable when someone cancels a coffee date, or do you believe that external causes prevented your friend from keeping her promise? The explanatory style works in the opposite direction, too. A pessimist believes that it was external luck that made them get a promotion, whereas optimists believe that it was an internal locus of control that got it. Explanatory style runs through three filters in the mind, also called the "three P's."

Optimists will use *permanence* so that bad events are temporary or external, and good events are permanent and internal. Pessimists have the opposite idea that bad events are permanent and internal, whereas good results are external and temporary.

Pervasiveness is another filter. An optimist realizes that a bad event is part of a specific cause, whereas pessimists believe that bad events are universal and life will never be positive again. Optimists also use pervasiveness to realize that the broader cause of good events is their competence. Pessimists explain the cause of a good outcome as having nothing to do with their efforts.

Personalization is another filter. Optimists will credit themselves for good results and recognize potential external factors for bad results, whereas pessimists will take sole responsibility for bad events and take no responsibility for well-deserved praise.

Be careful of optimism bias as well. Optimism bias is where you believe that everything will work out, no matter what. This leads to risky behavior because people with unrealistic optimism believe that nothing bad can ever happen to them. Would you really believe that smoking doesn't affect you because you're positive about it? What about drinking and driving? It's always good to consider all the factors, including the potential risks involved. Remember that luck has some influence in your life, but poor decisions and reckless behavior can lead to disastrous outcomes. You can't stop going to the doctor because you optimistically feel perfect.

You can't avoid wearing a seatbelt while driving or spending all your money on lottery tickets because you believe that you'll win. Adopt a realistic optimism because this can become a self-fulfilling prophecy when your mind is determined to reach your desired outcomes, but don't bank on nothing ever going wrong. Fortunately, there are two optimism tests you can easily find online to determine how realistic your optimism is.

The first one is called *The Learned Optimism Test*, which is derived from Seligman's work. It's a subjective questionnaire that includes 48 questions and you only have to choose the answer that is truest for you. You can't choose right or wrong answers, but the test will relatively measure how optimistic you are.

The second option is called *The Optimism Test*, which is another self-assessment that gives you an accurate score of your optimism proportion. There are 10 questions, and each scores you between zero and four, and will give you a percentage. Anything under 40 indicates that you're extremely pessimistic, anything between 40 and

80 indicates balanced optimism, and anything over 80 is extreme optimism with rose-colored goggles. Once you know how optimistic you are, tap into your realistic optimism to ensure that you don't take unwanted risks.

Learned Optimism

Not only can the optimism trait be learned; research has proven that it can also improve your overall health, increase motivation and performance, and it can pave the way to professional success (Moore, 2019c). Optimism decreases stress, eliminating the dangers that come when the body remains in a constant state of stress. The brain remains healthier, and so does the heart, arteries, and immune system. Peak functionality ensures that your mind and body remain healthy.

Balanced optimism or realism also encourages people to look after their health because bad things can happen to good people. Optimism improves your motivation and performance because it relies on intrinsic rewards in the brain. Improved happiness equals improved motivation. Being optimistic in your career is another intrinsic reward, and you become subjectively satisfied with your work. Indeed, you'll struggle for success in a job that offers no satisfaction.

Learning to become optimistic means that you must recondition the "three P's" through which every thought and response is filtered. Pessimists have distorted filters, and you'll need to overcome these distortions with simple exercises. Use the ABC technique to become aware of your filtered distortions first. 'A' stands for adversity, 'B' stands for belief, and 'C' is for consequence. The adversity is the problem you face, the belief is how you think you need to respond, and the consequence is what happens after you respond. The "three Ps" filter the progression from point A to point B. Being aware of your filters will already help you to replace them with different approaches.

Use one of the easy exercises to practice optimism once you're aware of your pessimistic distortions.

Musical Roles

Use this exercise to tap into the realistic side of optimism because it should allow you to see it from various perspectives, experience the good and the bad, and it gives your mind insight into the most realistic option because you'll experience the feelings involved in each outcome. Choose any situation where you're required to think positively or negatively. Perhaps, you need to choose a response to your friend turning down a lunch invite. Place two chairs across each other, and alternate between them. Each chair represents either the negative or positive side of the argument.

Imagine that you're two people for this exercise. Sit in the negative chair and determine the cause of the incident, how you feel about it, and what the deeper meaning is. Try to keep your cause internal, your feelings negative, and your meaning permanent. Now, switch chairs, and determine the same three factors, but you're in the positive chair now. Your cause needs to be external, your feelings positive, and your meaning must be temporary. Play the role of each mindset, and keep changing between the chairs until you recognize which chair makes you feel happier.

Challenge Your Thoughts

Create a worksheet where you have three columns. The first column is the thought that pops into your mind as soon as you're faced with adversity. You were late to pick your son up from school, so now, you think that you're a terrible mom. The second column is where you provide realistic evidence for why you were late. Keep in mind that you're practicing optimism, so keep the reasons external, temporary, and specific. It won't happen daily, it wasn't your fault that roadworks caused traffic, and your parenthood isn't defined by one incident. Now, record your alternative thought in the last column. Maybe you can say: "The roadworks held me up, but I can take a different route tomorrow because my response is within my control." Challenge your thoughts over the coming weeks, and notice how they change.

The Best Possible Self

Using your optimism to create a self-fulfilling prophecy is as simple as imagining your best self daily. Spend 10 minutes every day imagining a realistic future where you're flourishing in your desired ambitions. Be specific in this visualization, and engulf yourself in the emotions you'd feel at that moment. Perhaps, you envision yourself earning a promotion. It's realistic if you intend to perform at your best possible self. Imagine how you'd feel as your boss congratulates you. What will you be wearing? What will you hear, see, smell, and feel at this incredible time? Envisioning a positive future could encourage you to pursue it, increasing your performance and motivation.

An Unmeasurable Benefit of Optimism

Optimism and hope sound similar, but they're vastly different. Optimistic people believe that the world is changing to become a better place, but hopeful people believe that they can be a part of making the world better. They see themselves as a cog in the machine that drives shared happiness, success, and a good life. Hope requires more courage than being positive. It's the act of having faith in yourself and your abilities to help to create a better world. Hope can also be called advanced realism because you know that you need to play a part in making your future brighter. However, optimism is a precursor for hope, which is an invaluable benefit you can't be without if you want a good life.

Having hope is how you consciously want a better life. It can also make painful situations more bearable until things get better. Everyone has a hint of hope inside of them, but it's the courageous few who envision a better future to motivate the drive to get there. Hope offers something that even realistic optimism lacks. Hope implies that a better future is possible, and possibilities are better than nothing. Don't mistake hope for wishful thinking, either. It's realistic but motivational, inspirational, and positive. Hope keeps us moving forward, even in the face of adversity, depression, anxiety, and negativity.

It promotes happiness, well-being, courage, and resilience. You'll have the confidence to take baby steps in the right direction because effort is a major factor in positive living. Hope can also provide meaning for us, leading us to look for more inspiration and awe moments, which are positive emotions you need to adopt. Once you have meaning, knowing what truly matters to you will create new opportunities and set you on the path of incredible goals. Moreover, hope only multiplies when you encounter setbacks and confidently move past them.

Realistic optimism and hope will get the ball rolling toward the life you desire. Your mind becomes more susceptible to the coming changes.

Chapter 4:

Rethinking Your Behavioral Experiences

You've gained a few tools to change your thought habits, but what about your behavioral habits? Prophecies can only be fulfilled if you act on them. Some new behavioral habits must be explored to aid your journey. Being emotionally ready can't get you to a good life alone. We can't only think positively; we also need to apply positive intent to our behaviors. We need to rationally plan and execute the steps required to make the changes we desire.

Why the Mind and Body Connection Matters

The best way to assertively incorporate your positive lifestyle is to turn negativity into positive emotions by applying concrete actions. Even though the pursuit of positive thoughts alone can't establish a good life, you still need them because enjoying yourself in the present moment can harness well-being. The best way you can connect the mind and body to create incredible experiences is to look for them. Trying to push away unwanted thoughts could backfire, but seeking experiences that promote positive emotions can overturn the resistance toward change.

Positive experiences are used as coping mechanisms at first, but they'll become an integral part of your life with time. They'll become a part of you, whether you're practicing mindfulness, visualization, hobbies, or better posture. You can't control other people, their actions, evolution, or even mother nature, but you can control how you react to every change. So, why should you practice deep breathing as one example? Breathing reminds you that you can control your reaction when the situation loses control. You get to feel the connection between your mind and body, leading to improved positive emotions.

The experiences you must seek will be divided into mental and physical experiences. Mental experiences help you endure or enjoy a conversation with someone. Physical experiences are where you'll engage with every aspect of it to enjoy it on a deeper level.

Mental Experiences: Mindfulness

There's a range of mental experiences to learn so that you can attract positive emotions. Deep within every mind is pure and unconditioned awareness that we tend to lose when we grow older. It focuses aimlessly on problems, fears, goals, and desires. Our time is consumed by this mental plain, and we lose touch with a deeper sense of self. Our minds become too busy and noisy until we learn to practice mindfulness. Mindfulness allows us to tame the mind, silence the noise, organize the clutter, and find the deeper authentic self. Awaken the peaceful inner self that hides underneath the negative thoughts, emotions, and distortions.

Mindfulness empowers us to respond to the environment from a new place. You don't need to react from the preservation part of your mind to non-threatening situations anymore. Your inner self also knows that you can't solve every problem, however immediate it might be. You can't stop the pandemic, and you can't end global warming, but you could make small changes to slow global warming down. Mindfulness puts you in touch with what you can change right now by being in the present moment. There's only one place you can make changes, and that's here and now.

The Mindful Nation Report was published in 2015, and it aimed to prove mindfulness is a powerful adaptation (Stutton, 2020). The intention was to recognize whether mindfulness can decrease the effects of chronic illnesses, improve mental health, enhance creativity and productivity, and create a nation of flourishing people. It was also noted that living in the present moment is the most powerful trick. Being mindful is as simple as remaining in the present moment as a curious, compassionate, and non-judgmental entity that pays attention to the body, mind, and environment. Your awareness of feelings, thoughts, and sensations increase.

Psychologically, your appreciation and fulfillment of life, relationships, and work improve. Cognitively, attention, memory, problem-solving, and innovation increase. Physically, your immune system functions better, hypertension decreases, pain diminishes, and sleep improves. Mindfulness even enhances neuroplasticity. The insular cortex that lies between the prefrontal cortex and the midbrain improves activity. It develops through mindfulness with the release of a protein called brain-derived neurotrophic factor (BDNF). This protein protects the neuroplasticity, development, and survival of synapses between the conscious and positive minds.

Waking the inner self can mostly be achieved by staying in the present moment, and this allows you to practice being authentic. Your true self is also your subconscious mind, and opening this connection between the conscious and subconscious minds helps you to remind it who it is. There are three incredible ways to remind the authentic self of what it's capable of and what it values.

Affirmations

Affirmations confirm your authentic self, locus of control, integrity, values, and desires. Your self-identity is flexible; therefore, your subconscious mind can adopt a positive attitude. It has nothing to do with being perfect or exceptional, but rather about being competent and adequate. The integral part of communicating directly with your subconscious mind also reminds it that praise and acknowledgment for accomplishments are deserved. The Self-Affirmation Theory in psychology comes with many benefits, including reminding your true identity of what it values, how flexible it can be, and how it doesn't need to be perfect.

Teaching your inner self to evaluate the circumstances authentically reduces stress by confirming real threats to your core values, and you can convince it to respond with intentional change (Moore, 2019a). Moreover, self-affirmation can reduce rumination, which only leads to negativity, making it another valuable practice to become positive. It also makes us more resilient against negative emotions by reminding the inner self of its self-concept. Use self-affirmations daily in your mindful journey to remind your true identity of its incredibility. You can say:

"I choose to be positive because I have control over internal factors."

"I won't be defeated by external factors out of my control."

"I deserve recognition for the efforts I make."

"One mistake doesn't define my inner truth or values."

Creative Visualization

The subconscious mind doesn't rely on external input; it relies on internal thought processing from the conscious mind. It doesn't know how something feels unless you consciously let it know. It doesn't know the difference between imagined and genuine input. The subconscious mind is also the most literal entity you'll meet. It has no sense of humor, and it doesn't understand sarcasm. It can only process information in the present moment as it doesn't understand past or future tense, either. Communicating input from the conscious to the subconscious mind requires finesse. You need to be more specific and detailed when you give it information.

Using creative visualization is how you communicate with enough detail, sensations, and clarity for the subconscious mind to understand your input. The negative habits of the past don't disappear, but you start associating positive emotions with the new experiences. Three requirements make creative visualization highly effective. Firstly, you must truly desire the outcome so that your emotions can guide you. Secondly, you must believe that you can attain the outcome. Thirdly, you must accept the outcome in your visualization. Swap negative emotions and thoughts for positive images in your imagination because your subconscious mind doesn't know better.

Send out positive actions to bring positive energy back into your life. The benefits of creative visualization exceed positivity. It increases your focus on the right tasks and enhances your self-confidence. You'll experience joy, find new inspiration because the imagination has no limits, and even improve relationships. Psychologist Laura King explains that creative visualization can help you fulfill the prophecy of your best self, too (Carpenter, 2007). All it requires is six simple steps.

The first step is to set the mood for optimal relaxation and comfort. Take a hot bath before you sit in a comfortable chair with no distractions. Do everything in your power to make yourself most comfortable.

The second step is to enter a meditative state where your conscious and subconscious minds can communicate. Sometimes, this can be reached merely by focusing on slow and steady breaths. Remember that you awaken the inner self with intense focus in the present moment.

The third step is to begin your visualization once the mind is still. Take your time to create the most detailed image you can imagine. Clarify the goal for your inner self, and pay attention to the sounds, smells, sights, sensations, and even tastes that surround you in this vision. Focus on the positive sensations after your first date went well.

The fourth step is to hold onto the feelings and sensations you experienced in step three for a few minutes so that the subconscious mind recognizes them.

The fifth step reminds you to make this a daily habit. Enter the same visualization daily to amplify its influence.

The final step is to set your intentions to make this goal happen. Visualize the steps you'll take to reach it, and be as detailed as step three. Self-affirm your intent to make this happen, and give the subconscious mind evidence of how you're going to do it.

Meditation

Meditation and mindfulness are often confused for being the same things. Mindfulness is a mindset or quality you possess, whereas meditation is a physical practice. Meditation is only a small part of mindfulness and vice versa. Mindfulness can even be used as a psychological treatment, which is absent from meditation. Meditation also allows you to do and not do at the same time. An informal method of being mindful is eating, walking, and conversing mindfully while you remain in the present to experience everything in the environment. Formal mindfulness is when you intentionally practice mindfulness with meditation.

Meditation can be a separate form of therapy, and it includes intentional relaxation, keen focus, and the expansion of the consciousness to remove external distractions, and in some cases, your attention might be focused on negative emotions so that you can remove the power they hold over the subconscious mind. Emotions are similar to toddlers. The more attention you give them, the less they throw tantrums. You can't judge them, and there's no way to completely erase them, but you can allow them to pass and give the subconscious mind alternative emotions with intentional meditation practices. Meditation has proven a few significant benefits in a growing body of research (Korie Miller, 2019b).

The amygdala becomes less active after just two months of meditation, and the retention of new information is increased. Your attention and learning abilities are improved, and negative emotions, including social anxiety and unwanted self-beliefs are significantly decreased. Even your fitness levels improve, and this is partly due to improved motivation to lead a better life. Your immune system is boosted, your risk of degenerative disorders like Alzheimer's is reduced thanks to meditation, and you have a lower risk of obtaining addictive and negative behaviors. Meditation gives you a deep connection to the inner self, preventing it from becoming erratic and negative.

There are various options you can apply daily. It's recommended to meditate daily, and you'll mostly see the significant benefits after six weeks. Use guided meditation if you don't know how to do it with an application called *Headspace*. Breathing or focus meditations are also great options for beginners. All you have to focus on is one thing, such as your breathing. You must feel every movement in your body's frame and listen to the sound of air passing in and out. There's also mantra meditation where you repeat the sound of a specific word that vibrates your throat. Walking meditation is also possible where you simply walk a scenic route and absorb every part of the environment through your five senses.

Progressive muscle relaxation meditation is when you focus on tensing muscle groups throughout your body before you abruptly release the tension. Focus on the release, and it helps to start at one end of the body and work your way upward or downward. Mindful meditation is used to simply focus on what's happening in your body and mind after reaching a deeper level of relaxation. Turn it into a relaxing visualization by imagining yourself on a beach or in a forest, soaking up every sensation involved. You can even enjoy a bath where you focus on the sensations on your skin when you change the temperature or add bubbles. One thing you'll learn is that meditation can be done anywhere, any time.

You can meditate by focusing on any task, such as baking a cake, washing a car, or doing the laundry. As long as you're intentionally stimulating your senses, you're meditating on some level, formal or not. Two meditation types you'll learn more about in later chapters are called compassion meditation and gratitude meditation. Compassion meditation is essential for a positive life. It teaches you how to cultivate compassion for others and yourself, which are key factors in a good life. It also helps you to combat the negative emotions you'll encounter from thoughts you must overcome. You can't reach a positive life unless you learn to stop judging yourself, either.

Gratitude meditation is useful and necessary for a good life, too. It helps you flood your subconscious mind with new evidence that suggests you should be grateful for the life you have and stop ruminating on past failures. Gratitude is a key to happiness, positivity, and mindfulness.

Physical Experiences

Increasing your engagement mindfully toward any physical experience already boosts your mind and body connection. Whether this is done with hobbies that interest you, developing new skills you enjoy, or looking for a new job that better suits your passions if this is desired, you'll experience the connection. Get lost in the moment, lose yourself in time, and get carried away, but experience every aspect of what you're doing. This is also known as the flow state, which we'll focus on in chapter six. The secret is that you must enjoy the experience to reach complete engagement. Two physical experiences can magnify your positivity.

Laughter

Have you ever laughed hard enough to make your stomach hurt? Did you ever reach a point where you tried to stop laughing, but nothing could prevent the side-splitting, toe-curling response to someone's ridiculous joke? That's because laughter is a psychological and physical response to stimuli. It runs deep enough to bring physical and emotional changes. Nothing is more powerful in restoring the connection between your mind and body than a good laugh. Other than stress-relief, a better circulation that stimulates every organ, and the unexpected elevation of positive emotions and thoughts while you're laughing on the floor is only the tip of the iceberg.

Even smiles are attractive, mood changing, and contagious. Laughter boosts the immune system, lowers blood pressure, increases positivity, and can even make you look and feel younger (Stibich & Gans, 2020). It also exercises muscles for greater abs and releases endorphins in the brain to instantly switch your reward system on. A study published in *Europe's Journal of Psychology* also proves that having a sense of humor leads to greater success (Maiolino & Kaiper, 2014). There's an ocean of research to support the connection between humor, laughter, smiles, and endless benefits.

Humor allows you to weather challenges with greater ease, and the psychosocial benefits include meaningful relationships, which are a requirement to lead a good life. Humor is a character strength you need to experience mindfully. It has its own history of psychology and research. The first theory is called *The Relief Theory*, which means that you relieve tension as soon as you bend over laughing. The second one is called *The Superiority Theory*, which is understandably correct when you feel superior to anyone who has failed miserably at what you achieved. This isn't an arrogant disposition; it enhances your self-esteem.

The third theory is called *The Incongruity Theory*, and it considers how every person conceptualizes humor differently. This theory also helps you to laugh about an outcome you didn't expect instead of beating yourself up. The best news is that you're surrounded by humor and laughter. Watch funny videos, movies, and anything that gets a giggle. Share a funny fact about yourself with a friend, and don't forget to laugh at yourself once in a while. Attend stand-up comedy with friends because you're more likely to laugh in a group with the contagious factor. Moreover, always look for something to laugh about when you're faced with a serious situation. Just remember to engage in every giggle.

Posture

"Sit straight" is a common echo our parents used, but good posture is meaningful in our lives. The Kellogg School of Management and Stanford Graduate School of Business did a little digging to see if there was any truth in this echo (Cohen, 2011). The results showed that posture was more meaningful in the corporate world than ranking or position. There was also evidence that it promotes better behavior and thinking. Great posture exudes power, leadership, and confidence. There's a psychological effect when you sit and stand straight; it's not just about spine health. You feel more powerful and positive when you're in an open or expansive position, and other people can also pick up on your power vibes.

You also enhance your self-regulation when you practice being in control of your muscles. Good posture has also led to persistence, whereas poor posture increases your risk for helplessness. The most significant benefit of having good posture is that you make the best first impression, and this can open a world of new doors for you. There are a few ways to improve your posture. The correct office chair is essential, and you need to sit with your back straight, forehead raised, shoulders level with your back, and your feet must be flat against the ground. We spend most of our time behind laptops, so use the correct posture to make it stick.

The secret while you're sleeping, standing, or sitting is to keep your spine straight. Lie on your side and place a pillow between your knees to support your posture. Stand with your shoulders in line with your spine and your chest expanded. Your forehead and chin must be slightly elevated as this puts you in an expansive position. Your body must feel like it's in a natural position, forgoing any strain on your muscles and joints. Slouching isn't natural.

You have a myriad of ways to intentionally behave positively so that your mind and body are in sync. Now, you're ready to move onto the next phase.

Chapter 5:

Indulging in Gratitude

Understanding the effect that gratitude has on the mind and why a displeased mind can't develop is a key factor in your journey. A mind that lacks gratitude is closed to receiving incoming benefits, but a grateful mind is open to new and wonderful things. An appreciative mind always looks for the best in itself and others, and it understands concepts of preciousness and worthiness.

How Gratitude Works

Gratitude is a skill, emotion, and development. It's one of the most prominent emotions, but it's also a skill acquired in childhood. Helping, giving, sharing, and showing appreciation are just the tips of gratitude. Ingratitude is the worst kind of self-defeat anyone can possess. You need to be aware of the efforts that make yourself and others feel good. Gratitude benefits the giver and the recipient, but some people suffer from ingratitude, likely due to parents who never taught them how to be grateful. Gratitude is also an attitude, which further develops the skill. It's a positive trait that allows you to appreciate everything good in the world.

Ungrateful people lack this skill, and they can't see the favors bestowed upon them, even if it's having a roof over their heads. Life becomes self-centered, and the ingratitude leads to people not noticing kindness or favor, which makes them seek more from the people giving it. Ungrateful people easily cross the line to manipulate others because they want more. They're never satisfied with what already exists. The first pitfall of ingratitude is that you could suffer from chronic misery when you can't see the beauty in gestures, favors, and nature. It becomes harder for you to overcome emotional turmoil when you have nothing to look forward to, and you have a risk of fulfilling the despair prophecy.

You'll be condemned to social exclusion because people stop favoring you if you're ungrateful. Everyone wants to feel appreciated, including you. Showing ingratitude when someone does something special or even menial isn't going to make you happy. You'll miss all the amazing benefits of gratitude in a lonely and unwanted life. The power behind simple gestures of appreciation, such as saying thank you is incredibly significant. The emotion we call gratitude is a neurological process. A study published in the *Frontiers in Psychology Journal* found that morality and gratitude evoke the right anterior temporal cortex in the brain (Chowdhury, 2019c).

This part of your brain is also connected to the pleasure and reward centers, making gratitude another pleasurable behavior. Study participants who developed their gratitude also had a larger volume of grey matter in this region. The research also concluded that stress hormones are reduced, and the feel-good hormones are released. Rewiring this part of your brain will further enhance your inner happiness and positivity. Toxic emotions are discarded from the limbic system that tries to control your conscious thoughts. The structural changes that happen in the brain can even change the way you perceive yourself and the people around you.

You gain a strong awareness of the present, and your motivation is intrinsic. Individual benefits include increased satisfaction, sleep, resiliency, and the development of humility, wisdom, and patience. It has psychosocial benefits, too, such as increased work performance and satisfaction, better relationships, and self-efficacy. One of the most incredible health benefits is that it reduces inflammation around the heart when the immune system functions properly again (Kori Miller, 2019a). Stress and the immune system cause inflammation, even when there isn't a threat in the body, so reducing stress also leads to less inflammation.

Keeping a gratitude journal is the simplest exercise you can practice twice weekly or daily, whichever works for you. It brings all the individual and collective benefits to enhance every aspect of your life. Gratitude journaling only requires you to record three things you're grateful for each time. These entries can include someone who smiled at you, finishing a work project, the amazing meal you had last night, or the person who sleeps next to you. Gratitude also helps you to cope flexibly with adversity, increasing your resilience. We become complacent with what we already have, and we focus on the obstacles we need to overcome to get back to our lives, but what about enjoying the present moment?

There will always be a new challenge, so not focusing on the things you already possess through gratitude is like tying a 50-pound weight to each ankle. Emotional resilience has five components. You need social competence to stand out from the people who are racing against the same ambitions. You need problem-solving to pay attention to the solutions you can proactively use to overcome challenges. You need autonomy to practice your internal motivation. You need forgiveness to let go of negative thoughts. You need empathy to see other people's perspectives. However, gratitude is the sixth trait of resilience. Building your emotional resilience is done with gratitude exercises.

For example, gratitude lists require two columns, one for the people you're thankful, and another one for the reasons why you're grateful. Include ten people and favors you're grateful for before writing thank you notes. Then, give these thank you notes to the people on your list. All in all, focusing on the good things in life, however small, also increases emotional resilience. Start seeing a glass as half full instead of half empty. Gratitude also has immense benefits in your relationships, it enhances the perceived quality of relationships for you and the other person. Who doesn't want to feel appreciated and loved?

You can't show someone how much you love them unless you appreciate them daily. Gratitude promotes a deeper kind of love by improving your conflict resolution skills, too. It's easier to resolve conflict when two people appreciate each other. Love, closeness, intimacy, and trust are increased between two people when each one perceives that the other person is attending to their needs and wants through appreciation. Romantic relationships can flourish, and your social attitude will create meaningful friendships.

Assessing Gratitude

It's good to have a baseline to work from before improving your gratitude. *The Gratitude Questionnaire* is also called the *GQ-6 Scale,* and it's the most popular online self-assessment. It measures your responsiveness, attitude, frequency, density, and expression. You'll answer questions where you have to choose an option between "strongly agree" and "strongly disagree." Your overall score will range between six and 42, with the intention of being closer to 42. You could try *The Gratitude Resentment and Appreciation Test (GRAT),* designed by Psychologist Phillip Watkins in 2003 (Kelly Miller, 2019).

The *GRAT* option measures your dispositional gratitude on a 44-question scale according to three distinct characteristics of a grateful person, such as your sense of deprivation, appreciation tendency, and expression. The *GRAT* scale is a reliable version, and there's also a revised version that only contains 16 questions. Most of the self-assessment tests measure your understanding of gratefulness, emotions behind it, attitude toward it, and your expression of it. Other tests include the *Gratitude Adjective Scale (GAC)* and *Functionality Appreciation Scale (FAS).*

Practicing Gratitude

Gratitude has no limits. You can be thankful for having functional legs, being religious, science, food, work, people, patience, or a willingness to learn. You can't keep your thankful ideas for Thanksgiving anymore. Make time for gratitude daily, even if it means committing to smiling at five strangers today. All that matters is that you're making a difference in your attitude, and watch how it returns to you as positive energy always does. A fun fact is that the 21st of September is Gratitude Day, so adopt habits to make it count next time. Various methods will exercise gratitude.

Journaling

People don't always know what to write, especially if you're teaching yourself to be grateful when you weren't before. Remember that your journaling is personal, and it can be records of people you're grateful for, things that make you smile, self-improvements, and your kindness to another person. These weekly prompts should help you get started.

- What have you done to make yourself grateful?
- What has someone else done to make you grateful?
- Are there any skills you learned that can be appreciated?

- What emotions made you feel grateful, such as love, patience, and someone else's appreciation?
- Which words spoken to you make you feel grateful?
- What words have you spoken to feel appreciation?
- What sensations did you experience to make you smile, such as taste, smell, touch, sight, and sound?

These prompts can guide you, but remember to be mindfully present in your writing. Record everything and every detail as you remember it.

Appreciate People

Appreciating someone else ranges from small acts of kindness, gentle advice, to treating them with respect. Respecting someone is an act of appreciation. Always respect people, even if they're a stranger. Be mindful of your words, and offer help where you can. Volunteering at the homeless shelter or a pet rescue facility can encourage gratitude. You need to appreciate the role that everyone has in this world by respecting their boundaries, honoring their hard work, and sharing their accomplishments with them. Don't forget to tip the waiter when you enjoy a nice meal with someone you appreciate and can be grateful for.

Quick Boosters

Actions speak loudly when you show people how much you appreciate their presence and favors in your life. Saying it is as simple as "thank you for being a great person." Start making homemade gifts because the effort put into them is appreciated more than a $100 gift card. Give people gifts just because you appreciate their help and relationship instead of waiting for the holidays. Visit them to thank them for something they said or did. While you're focusing on them, listen actively when you ask them how they are. Active listening is appreciated by mist. Why not increase your gratitude attitude at home by making a scrapbook that your family creates together?

A Gratitude Challenge

A 21-day gratitude challenge helps if you're new to being grateful. Create a structured plan, which includes a few prompts daily. Mornings are our most focused time of the day, so start your day by standing in front of the mirror and asking yourself what you're grateful for. Your next task is to write one unique thing you're grateful for today, such as something you saw that is out of the ordinary. This part of the challenge encourages you to look for appreciated beauty. Add a session of gratitude meditation to your daily tasks, and commit to saying thank you at least once a day. Spend 10 minutes at night to recap the day's gratitude. These prompts are simple and flexible enough to suit anyone.

The Gratitude Jar

Decorate a jar or box with stickers, ribbons, and whatever you fancy. Recognize three things you're grateful for daily, write them on a colorful piece of paper, and put them in your jar. With time, your jar fills up, and you'll realize that you have at least a group of reasons to be thankful.

The Appreciation Rock

This exercise seems silly to some, but pick up a beautiful rock from the beach, and place it in a different place every day. Place it on your partner's pillow in the morning if this is what your appreciation focus is for the day. Appreciating the fact that you have a car to get around means that you can put it on your console for the day. Keep moving the rock to places and objects you're grateful for.

Gratitude Meditation

The most powerful form of disciplined and committed gratitude you can practice daily is meditation. It's a conscious effort to appreciate things, and it helps you reflect on people and things you might've overlooked. Practicing it when the day comes to an end helps you pay tribute to your ability to survive the day, including its challenges. Your main focus for this meditation type will be gratitude. Combining intentional gratitude with meditation can show the subconscious mind how many things you have to be grateful for. It will bestow the benefits of gratitude on the subconscious mind, such as better health, social awareness, positivity, and happiness. Gratitude meditation also helps you to focus on negative experiences while you look for reasons why you need to be grateful for them.

For example, focus on your accident that broke your leg. What could you be grateful for in this scenario? You're certainly grateful that you were wearing a seatbelt that saved your life! Gratitude meditation is enhanced with four elements. It must be a consistent daily practice, and it requires the right space and time to optimize it. Keep your space quiet from distractions, and meditate in the morning while your mind is most focused. Posture is another element that enhances meditation. Assuming the easy yoga pose with your legs crossed, spine straight, hands rested, and chin raised is a good start. The fourth element is that you're not allowed to judge yourself, especially when you focus on negative events to find reasons for gratitude.

Add a few mantras to your session to increase its intensity. *Karuna Hum* means that you accept kindness and compassion, *Namaste* means that you welcome everyone, *Dhanyavad* means thank you, and *Kritanja Hum* means that you're grateful. Guided sessions on *Headspace* must be chosen for gratitude efficiency, but you can also use simple steps to practice gratitude meditation yourself. Whether you meditate for five or 20 minutes, these steps will guide you.

Step one reminds you to assume a comfortable position that supports your expansive posture. Lying on a bed or sitting in front of a window to nature also works.

Step two is to enter the meditative state again. Choose something to focus on, such as your breathing, a dot on the ceiling, or the mantra you're using.

Step three is where you start painting a picture. Design a memory if you want to find a reason for appreciation, or you can imagine someone's face in front of yours. You can even play the memory of how you navigated the day, or you can keep it simple by focusing on the amazing meal you had. Paint a detailed picture that opens your senses to the experience.

Step four is when your picture is complete. Pay attention to the sensations you feel while you're watching this movie play. Look at the colors, listen to the sounds, and smell the pretty flowers you pass on the road. It was a long journey to reach your destination, and you're tired now.

Step five is where you identify a reason to be grateful. The journey was long indeed, but you got here safely. You arrived in a beautiful place with incredible sensory stimuli without any troubles on the way. The biggest challenge was boredom, but there are many reasons to be grateful. Focus on these reasons for at least five minutes, playing them over and over in your mind while you allow the sensations to engulf you.

That's all you need to complete a gratitude meditation session. The time you stay in this reminiscent state is up to you, but practice some form of gratitude meditation daily.

Yoga is another connection to gratitude. You become one with nature, which is an integral part of appreciating what nature brings. The yogic lifestyle encourages the appreciation of your health, body, and mind so that you can lead a long and prosperous life. Gratitude yoga allows us to express our gratefulness to ourselves and other people through gestures and movements. You face challenges with an open heart instead of hiding from them because there's always something to be grateful for. Gratitude yoga uses mudras, which are hand movements that redirect energy back into our minds and bodies.

It's a gesture of offering, which is one definition of gratitude. Asanas are the physical postures you assume in yoga to open your body and mind to feelings of gratefulness and contentment. The most popular asanas for gratitude are the child, camel, mountain, and corpse pose. Gratitude yoga requires five elements from you. You need to intend gratefulness, be committed to receiving it, make every movement count by practicing it with a trained coach, maintain your focus, and stay grounded in the present moment.

Kindness, Understanding, and Gratitude

Kindness is another essential part of gratitude, and it comes with many similar benefits. It depresses negative emotions by releasing positive hormones, and it boosts confidence in yourself and others. Moreover, kindness produces the love hormone oxytocin, which is good for the heart (Proctor, 2017). The truth is that people are unlikely to treat you any less than how you treat them, and living a good life means that community also matters. You can't be happy if your relationships are dysfunctional, but kindness and understanding promote better relationships. The smallest act of kindness has the potential to make a difference in someone's life, even your own.

It encourages people to treat you kindly, and it promotes a sense of control and optimism. Kindness also gives you a sense of belonging in the community when you volunteer or help someone. Seeing the small changes when you're kind to someone helps you to rewire your brain. Just remember that being kind to people doesn't mean that you must put your morals and desires on the backburner. It must never be a way for people to manipulate you because then you're dealing with ungrateful people. Their toxic ungratefulness will become yours if you allow them to manipulate you. Always be kind in ways you enjoy while keeping other people's feelings in mind. Never hurt someone intentionally, and don't overdo it.

Volunteer work is a great option to practice kindness. Become a mentor for struggling youth. Sign up for extra-curricular duties at your child's school, or offer skillshare over Zoom. Call a friend you haven't chatted with in a while, donate clothes to a charity, or pay for someone's groceries at the checkout. Plan a fundraiser for a youth group, or send flowers to someone who received bad news. Shop for the elderly, or hand out a few thank you notes to people who need some kindness. Compliment a stranger, or offer a colleague help with their presentation.

However, it's as important to show yourself kindness as it is to share it with other people. Self-compassion is required to complete a good life, and we'll focus on this in chapter eight. Whether you're forgiving yourself, respecting yourself, or doing what you love, kindness enhances your journey. Gratitude, kindness, and learning to appreciate everything you once ignored already makes your life seem so much more enjoyable. Now, it's time to adopt a flow state, which increases your outlook tenfold.

Chapter 6:

Experiencing Flow

Positive psychology brings us one more tool to use—the flow state. It's considered the height of engagement and happiness. Being so lost in an experience brings you closer to living a good life, but you need to know what it is, what benefits it brings, and how to achieve it. It's not entirely a matter of losing yourself in an experience. It goes beyond that. There's an exact science behind it, and it is an essential part of your journey if you want to find authentic happiness in your positive life.

Introducing Flow

A name that many people find impossible to pronounce is Mihaly Csikszentmihalyi, but he's the second founding father of positive psychology, and more importantly, he's the first person to study the science behind flow (Oppland, 2019). Overcoming the tongue twister can be done by pronouncing his name phonetically. Mihaly is pronounced as "me high," and Csikszentmihalyi "chicks send me high." It all started when Hungarian-born Csikszentmihalyi wanted to understand happiness after World War Two removed it from the world.

There was only pain, suffering, and loss, and happiness became a distant goal. He was interested in religion, philosophy, and art at the time he visited Switzerland, and he happened to attend a lecture by Swiss Psychologist Carl Jung at the ski resort. Suddenly, Csikszentmihalyi realized that psychology could help him find answers to what makes a life worth living so that people's happiness can be restored. He came to America to study psychology, and his life quickly intertwined with Seligman, but it wasn't until a fascinating epiphany that Csikszentmihalyi became known as the co-founder of PP.

The epiphany happened when Csikszentmihalyi watched musicians play their instruments, albeit these musicians were talented enough to create complex music that still soothed the minds and hearts of their audience. He was intrigued by the psychology behind what he saw now that he understood the human mind better. He watched these musicians enter "the zone" where nothing other than themselves and their experience existed. It's as though they became one with their experience. The music flowed through them, but they flowed through the rhythms simultaneously. Csikszentmihalyi saw a new kind of happiness in these musicians.

Csikszentmihalyi wanted to explore whether the psychology of this "zoned participation" was related to a life worth living. He researched alongside Seligman to understand how these musicians enter the flow state and how they could use this as inspiration to allow regular people to enter the same flow that's constantly moving throughout our lives. Every moment in time is an ever-moving experience, and what would happen if we could enter this experiential flow? It wasn't long before Csikszentmihalyi understood that this flow state existed across genders, cultures, professions, ages, classes, and activities. Many people experience flow without even realizing it. They get lost in time, albeit at the present moment, and their performance is exceptional.

Csikszentmihalyi's earlier studies already proved that happiness was internal. It didn't rely on external beings and factors. Moreover, this intrinsic happiness can be manipulated by entering the flow state. However, it requires intention and commitment. He described flow as the intense desire to continue doing what you're busy with because the experience is so enjoyable that you can't even be distracted by challenges. His work eventually concluded that the flow state is marked by six factors.

Firstly, you become intensely focused, with every fiber of your being, on the experience in the present moment.

Secondly, your actions and awareness merge to push out any potential ruminations or objections.

Thirdly, you lose your self-consciousness or notice the lack of attention to yourself.

Fourthly, you have a strong sense of control in your experience.

Fifthly, your sense of time becomes distorted in a way that makes hours pass in minutes.

Finally, you experience intrinsic motivation to continue the experience, even if it's challenging.

It's not a flow state without these six factors, and anyone can reach it. Research published in *The Journal of Personality and Individual Differences* explains that certain personality types enter the flow easier, but anyone is capable of entering it with the right intentions, persistence, and understanding (Ullén et al., 2012). People with an autotelic personality type will experience it more. This personality type includes anyone who relies on internal goals and not external desires. It also includes people with meta-skills, including persistence, low self-centeredness, and a high passion for life.

The least likely personality to enter the flow state is the neurotic type of self-centered people who have perfectionist tendencies. Whatever your personality type might be, you can still learn to enter the flow state. You're reading this book, which already means that you have a high interest in life, even if it's new. Practicing gratitude and compassion already guides you away from self-centeredness, which you've learned how to practice. Persistence is the only skill you're possibly lacking, but guess what? It's a learned and chosen skill. You aren't born persistent; you choose to persevere.

There are two neurological confirmations during flow according to Associate Professor of Psychology Arne Dietrich at the American University of Beirut in Lebanon (Oppland, 2019). The prefrontal cortex goes into temporary hibernation, also referred to as transient hypofrontality, which is what lifelong Buddhists achieve in transcendental meditation. The conscious mind gives way to the subconscious mind to experience the event or task. It's the highest form of transcendence, even by professional standards. It's also the deepest form of allowing the subconscious mind to experience external sensations and joy for itself.

Transcending to a higher mind is how you lose time and self-consciousness, but it also silences the inner critic because your inner self and everything you value and believe takes center stage. This process also allows the wider brain to activate, leading to higher creativity and productivity. Moreover, there's a constant flow of happy hormones flooding through your brain while you're lost in transcendence.

Why It Matters

Giving your subconscious mind power through transience leads to endless benefits. It's like spoon-feeding it with the correct information to push rumination right out of the door. You become fully alert, and your focus is energized on a new level. Performance peaks because your focus isn't divided with distractions, leading to improved work performance and accomplishments. The human brain is only capable of processing 120 bits of information per second according to Csikszentmihalyi, and reaching the flow state uses most of this capacity (Firefly, 2017). It also takes the brain about 60 bits per second to process language when someone speaks to you, and this helps you understand why the flow state can block out distractions. There just isn't space for them.

You also find the strength to overcome challenges because the flow state requires difficulty or you won't reach it. Challenges need to peak your attention, and having the focused energy required to overcome obstacles in your experience is what gives you the additional skill of masterful problem-solving. Not only can you learn new skills; you can also master them, and you can do so quickly. You also get to pay attention to what really matters the most to you, and this multiplies your intrinsic motivation to keep moving forward. Flow even increases your resilience when you rise to challenges instead of avoiding them. Moreover, you reach a stage of eustress, which is the state in which you can positively respond to stress.

Eustress is when the brain responds to stress with positive emotions and hormones, and this pushes you toward a fulfilled life with meaning and hope. With positive responses in the brain, negative emotions and thoughts can't consume you, improving mental health and reducing depression, anxiety, and stress. Besides, being so engulfed in the experience doesn't leave much room for negativity. In time, the subconscious mind adopts positive thinking because it has a chance to experience the sensations first-hand.

The Basics

There are some well-known secrets to achieving the flow state. It's key to note what you can't allow during your pursuit of flow. There should be no distractions because they rob your attention of transient focus, disrupting the experience. Modern life is fast-paced, and it's difficult to find a time without distractions, but you can't reach flow without doing this first. A first step is as simple as switching off your smartphone, disconnecting the Wi-Fi, or wearing noise-canceling headphones. Close the windows so you can't hear traffic, or find white noise to play softly in the background. The simplest steps can remove distractions if you consciously intend to reach the flow state.

The second secret is to choose an experience you find interesting or love. It helps to be good at the task, or at least be trained well enough to enter flow. You can't expect to pick up a violin if you've never touched one before. Be realistic in the activities you choose for flow. Having enjoyable activities that you have some control over through practiced skills is one part of this secret. Also, ensure that the task offers some challenge to you. Boredom is the fastest way you can exit the flow state, and it doesn't help to improve your skills anyway. Choose an activity that is higher than your skill by just enough to offer a challenge. Don't choose one that makes your brain retaliate with stress and doubt.

The third secret is to know what the motivation of your flow is. You need to offer the conscious mind motivation to allow the hibernation that wakes the subconscious mind. Consciously reflect on what the flow state means to you, how it will improve your life, and set your intentions before the activity. The motivation offered must be intrinsic. Extrinsic motivation is when people pursue money or fame, and this only offers short-term motivation, which doesn't help you transcend.

These three secrets ensure a state of flow if you consciously intend to reach the six factors required to define a transcendent state.

Transcending Into Flow

The flow state puts a foot in the door of eudaimonia, and some methods can increase the chance of achieving it. The flow state completes two segments of the PERMA model pie. It offers engagement on a new level, but it can enhance your sense of accomplishment as well. Exploring a sense of accomplishment happens every time you reach a goal, milestone, or even engage in something meaningful and enjoyable. It's also achieved when you reach the flow state, but it isn't entirely reliant on it. Simply having ambitions and goals in life can help you feel accomplished, but using the PERMA model to design goals can improve your chances of reaching them.

Your goals need to be meaningful and realistic to make them count as part of this undeniable pursuit. Having realistic goals is how you design life between anxiety and boredom. One that challenges you enough to reach a flow state, but it isn't too challenging to make you anxious. An effort toward realistic goals will already give you a sense of satisfaction, and you'll experience fulfillment, actualization, eudaimonia, and pride when you accomplish goals that are achievable and mean everything to you. Accomplishment is a human requirement to thrive and flourish. So, set your goals before you try to enter a flow state. Consider which activities, new skills, or talents can push you over the accomplished line. You'll learn more about meaningful goals in chapter seven.

Another method of transcending into a flow state is to visually expose yourself to what you want. Take sports as an example because athletes commonly enter flow during a race. You might not have what it takes to reach flow yet unless you've been training enough. Perhaps, you want to cycle. Visual stimuli are a powerful tool in any ambition. You have to start training, but you can surround yourself with images of the Tour de France and other cycling events around the world. Watch videos of how you can enhance your aero dynamism, and apply them in your training. More importantly, push yourself a little harder every time you train. Challenge yourself to be an ounce better than your last session. Keep it realistic, but a challenge is required to prevent boredom.

You can use visual stimuli in any scenario to enhance your intrinsic motivation as long as the activity is something you desire. Maybe you want to become a musician. Surrounding yourself with images is one way to complement your practice, but you can also use creative visualization to store the images deep in your subconscious mind, preparing it for transcendence. Visualize your goals daily, and engage with your senses while you imagine a scenario where you flourish in your talents. Remember that goals must be realistic, so don't choose to be a musician unless you have a base talent for it. Some people don't have the cognitive abilities required for music. Talent is a skill you develop, but it's not easily developed without a base. Choosing a flow potential where the challenge outweighs the skills won't work.

Skills are another ambitious option to attempt to reach a flow state. Your creativity and productivity are enhanced during the flow state, meaning that you'll learn these skills faster. What have you always wanted to learn? Choose something you're passionate about. Nothing stands in your way of learning new skills because the online world provides material for just about anything. Are you passionate about psychology? Research the various types, models, and theories because you might find one that can be used as a long-term passion. For example, hypnosis stirs your curiosity, and you research everything you need to know, including the neuroscience behind it. You can do a short course to license yourself as a hypnosis instructor.

Guiding someone into the subconscious mind is quite an accomplishment, and you can reach the flow state with any activity you choose. Some people enjoy their work, but they don't have the skills they need to double their production. Let's say that you're a writer. You've stuck to nonfiction for years, and the research serves you well. However, you've always wondered how fiction writing would feel. Sometimes, you find yourself getting lost in the flow of your words, but your flow is frequently interrupted by research. People want facts and studies, but this limits the amount of flow you can reach. It could even prevent flow. Sign up for a few courses that help you learn how to write dialogue, and practice your skill until you can enter the flow of losing yourself in a fictional world.

Keep in mind that every time the challenge becomes easier, you need to kick it up one notch to make it challenging again. It doesn't matter what activity you choose to practice flow as long as you meet the six factors, and use the three secrets to maintain it. Start a woodwork project, build a treehouse, or take up a new hobby. Give yourself time to master the skill enough to reach flow. Don't expect yourself to attain the flow state if you reach for stars unrealistically beyond your grasp. Optimism also teaches you to be realistic. Combine what you've learned this far, and pursue internal goals. Forget about what society wants. Forget about what your friends think you love. Focus on what you enjoy, and this will lead to mastery, which leads to flow. Finding meaning in your life and applying it to everything you've learned is the next phase of your journey.

Chapter 7:

Believe in Yourself and Acknowledge Your Potential

The positivity starts pouring in once you know what you want from life because you know what direction you're heading in, and you have a clear idea of which path leads there. You may find setbacks and obstacles on your path, but that's okay. Now that you're armed with all the tools from the previous chapters, you'll know how to navigate through them. Purpose and positive thinking go hand in hand in that respect; you can't embrace positive thinking without some kind of purpose, nor will you accomplish your purpose without positive thinking.

Purpose and Happiness

Without purpose, there's no happiness, and without happiness, there's no purpose to live a worthy life.

Positive psychology aims to find out how we can live a life worth living. *The Journal of Positive Psychology*, headed by well-known Psychologist Roy Baumeister, published the research behind a good life, which includes meaning and happiness (Baumeister et al., 2013). Happiness is required to live a life worth living, but it's a flawed desire without purpose. Happiness doesn't automatically lead to meaning, and vice versa. Positive emotions alone can't elicit a fulfilling and satisfying life.

Happiness is a present moment experience, but the meaning is focused on the past and future influence over the present moment. You can use meaningful influence by considering the past and future while finding happiness in the present. It's like a double-edged sword of guaranteed contentment. Focusing on what you want and need boosts happiness. However, you might have to supplement your focus to find meaning and happiness simultaneously. This can be supplemented in three ways.

Firstly, understand that givers and takers feed different sides of this paradox. Takers experience short bursts of happiness in the present moment, but it lacks meaning. Givers experience meaning behind their actions, so you need to give back to other people to achieve a purpose. You must give and accept the generosity other people share with you.

Secondly, you must be authentic to find a purpose. Intentionally expressing your authentic self and having a sense of personal identity are purposeful, but they offer no happiness. Find a purpose if you lack it by being authentic with your boundaries, values, goals, passions, and beliefs. Add happiness to authenticity by seeking it in the present.

Finally, negative emotions serve a purpose in a meaningful life. Indeed, a life high in purpose and low in happiness could be susceptible to anxiety, stress, and depression; however, having a strong sense of meaning with a hint of negative emotions can drive your motivation to pursue the life you want.

Listen for a Calling

Finding a purpose seems insurmountable to many people, but often, it stares them in the face. The main question is what makes you tick? What do you feel passionate enough about to defend it at any cost? Look at your subscriptions, Facebook groups, books, movies, hobbies, and the skills that captivate you. For example, Joe can't define his purpose, yet, his bookshelf is packed with engineering books, his favorite programs include The Big Bang Theory and Mythbusters, and he's part of over a dozen Facebook groups covering different aspects of inventions and scientific advancements.

Joe still wonders what his purpose is as he needs to choose his major. Every hint of his purpose stares at him, Joe could find his niche in science. He can invent something that makes his life worth living, and it makes other people's lives easier. Look at your present life, and find signs of captivation. Sometimes, it isn't only about what excites and inspires you. Things that enrage you also work. Maybe you're enraged by the hunger in Africa, and you can join an organization that allows you to make a difference. Four steps can help you find your calling.

Step one is to take an inventory of past inspiration. What have older purposes taught you? Either they remain alive, or you realize that they weren't meaningful to you.

Step two is to create a meaningful journal. Keep journaling about your calling every morning until you feel that you've found the right one. Ask yourself what your calling is, and write down 50 answers before you can think, edit, or pause.

Step three is to create a poll for your friends and family once you have a list of five passions from step two. Keep in mind that your purpose is personal, so you don't have to take their advice, but it helps to ask our loved ones what they think of our chosen passions. They might remind us that we're germaphobes, so Africa is an unrealistic dream.

The final step is to allow your values to guide you. List the core values that make you authentic, forgoing the qualities you possess in a future vision. What qualities and values do you have right now? You can always learn new qualities, but driving 1,000 miles on half a tank of gas isn't realistic. Even though you plan to gain the qualities you need; you still need to get to the nearest gas station first.

Forget about what other people want for or of you. Indeed, you ask for advice if you're stuck, but your passions shouldn't line someone else's expectations. Forget about monetary, societal, embarrassing, and judgmental concepts. Answering your call isn't difficult once you know what you want. Work on your self-limiting beliefs to create a positive mindset with the exercises in this book. Self-limiting beliefs sabotage your adoption of a purpose, and the biggest downfall comes from perfectionism. You might fail at one or two meaningful pursuits. Indeed, you can have many at once, but don't allow yourself to stand in your way.

It also helps to reconnect with your 'why' from time to time because humans tend to lose motivation with time. Goals require you to know your 'why,' so remind yourself often of why you find your pursuit meaningful. This also allows you to make the sacrifices often needed. You have a vision, and this vision is how your life must play out. Establishing realistic and intelligent goals can also help you proceed, especially when it's hard to start. You might have other full-time commitments, and you'll need to plan your vision to make it work. You'll know when you've made it work. Obstacles will simply fade into the journey, and you'll experience a feeling like no other. You'll be at ease with your progress.

Two philosophies make this journey easier as well. The "just do it" philosophy teaches us to simply start our journey. The fear of failure and perfectionism make us hesitate before we take the first step. It's not always healthy to overthink things because this only causes procrastination and lost opportunities. Moreover, seemingly insurmountable changes will only intensify or overwhelm you where the possibility exists if you wait.

Force yourself to take a leap of faith, even if it's one tiny step.

That illuminates the second philosophy of "doing it step-by-step." You don't need to leap 50 yards at once; you simply need to take a baby step. Change takes time, and answering your calling is a huge change, which can take years. So, your question now is how do you pursue what you want? Having goals is the answer.

Set Goals

Goals are the plans we make to improve the future with inspiration from the past, and the desires we have in the present. It allows us to connect to each passage of time to ensure success. Interesting facts about setting meaningful goals include intrinsic motivation that drives better performance and reaching the flow state (Houston, 2019b). Shockingly, around 25% of students never complete their studies and they explain that they didn't set clear goals. Hope and optimism can also increase your chances of reaching your ambitions, and specific, challenging goals improve your chance of success.

Social influence has also had a significant impact on goals, but specific goals are driven by a passion to learn more and offer enough intrinsic value to prevent negative social influence. The most incredible fact about meaningful goals is that they're more motivational than money. To guarantee goal success and enjoyment, they need to contain five principles.

You must be committed and determined to reach your goal, which isn't a problem if it provides meaning and happiness. You need clarity to define specific goals, and this keeps you on a direct path to some form of success.

The goal also needs to be challenging but achievable enough to reach the flow state. Challenging goals improves performance, leading to better internal satisfaction. The task complexity must also be realistic. Complex goals that shadow your skills aren't recommended. The complexity also includes a realistic time-factor. Don't aim for the chief executive officer in one year if you're currently in the mailroom. The third and fourth principles coexist to some extent. The final principle is that your goals require immediate feedback. Feedback allows us to readjust our sights if the target has moved or if our skills fall shy of the target.

This can often be achieved by reviewing your goals frequently. Have two sets of goals, long-term and short-term, but review both columns every four weeks for optimal benefits. Three goals are a good number to start with. Have one two-year goal, one six-month goal, and one 30-day goal. Too much gusto causes burnout, and your shorter goals will change every month anyway. Have milestones for every goal, including the 30-day one, which keeps topping up your motivation when you unlock progress. It's also essential to have positive goals. Don't list a goal like "I want to stop eating junk-food" just because your purpose is to help American youth become fit.

This is a negative goal that comes with negative emotions. Rather change the goal to "I want to lead a healthier lifestyle to be a role model for these kids." This isn't very specific, but it makes a point. Goals don't need to be for specific outcomes, either. Set goals to gradually increase the intensity of your weekly workout. Start with 25 minutes today and switch to 30 minutes by next Monday. There's nothing you can't set goals for, including meaning, new skills, and change. One of the greatest methods to prevent goals from making you doubt yourself when you stumble is to be flexible.

Never set your goals in stone. Indeed, they must be specific, but your monthly reviews also show you potential improvements. You can't improve unless you're flexible. Nevertheless, there's one acronym to remember whenever you set goals—SMART.

The 'S' reminds you to be specific in every goal and milestone. You must be able to see yourself take action toward a milestone. Take the example of being a fitness role model. Close your eyes, and watch yourself take actionable steps to each milestone that leads to the outcome. What will you do in week one? What needs to be done in week two? Lay down all the cards, and include sensations in your actionable visualization.

The 'M' stands for measurable, and breaking your goal into at least four steps or milestones helps you measure your progress. Each step needs to be as specific as the original goal, and it helps to review your monthly goal weekly to make sure you're stocking up on enough motivation.

The 'A' means attainable, and you need to consider your skills, abilities, and qualities. Can the "role model" person genuinely be one if they have no social skills? Could they show young kids how to eat better and exercise if they suffer from social anxiety? They could take a public speaking course to overcome anxiety, but this goal isn't attainable unless this is part of their specific milestones. Remember that you need a challenge, but you also don't need a guaranteed failure.

The 'R' stands for relevancy, and you must determine whether the goal is relevant to the purpose you chose. Sticking to the example used, the "role model pursuer" can't say that learning to become faster on the track is relevant to her pursuit. She intends to help get young people fit by being an example who talks to them in a group session. She could use her track times as inspiration, but they're not entirely relevant to her goal. Every milestone must be relevant.

The 'T' stands for time-factor, and you need to give every goal a time to start and end, including the milestones. This helps you track your progress in your reviews.

Be reasonable with your purpose and any other goals you choose. Moderation is key because you can't overwhelm yourself, either. It's wonderful to find something you're passionate about, but making drastic and sudden changes without preparing the field is a disaster. Take risks, but not enough to destabilize yourself.

The Required Skills

Having a purpose is incredible, but you need to adopt a few skills to ensure success in your journey.

Failure Reconstruction

People are conditioned to fear failure throughout childhood. It makes us doubt ourselves, and it's an emotional punch to the gut. Embrace failure to pursue your purpose. Mistakes come with lessons, and making them means that you've made an effort. Reframe your idea of failure by remembering that you attempted something other people hesitate with. An effort outweighs regret when you choose not to do anything. Failure promotes self-growth because you'll never learn what your limits or shortcomings are unless you try. Take a weightlifter as an example, he increases his weight frequently until he reaches his limit.

He finally pushes the maximum weights he can lift, and often, his attempt temporarily injures him, but he knows what he can do, and it doesn't make him give up. He trains until his muscles grow stronger, allowing him to lift more weight. Before anything, admit that you fear failure, and then you can learn to grow from it. Your self-resilience also grows, making you more comfortable with failure in the future, which allows you to explore new strengths. Failure should inspire you; it must make your desires burn hotter because you don't know what opportunity lies ahead unless you embrace it. Imagine an incredibly emotional experience when success comes after mistakes.

Self-Reliance

Self-reliance is the trust you possess in your abilities, judgment, and decisions. It's the ability to rely on yourself to fulfill a good life or to find a purpose. It doesn't shun society or rely on it, but it allows internal authenticity to drive your purpose train. It's the ability to confidently think autonomously. Believing in your skills and purpose and knowing that it has merit is how you succeed. You get to embrace your individuality before bravely taking the steps required to reach your dreams. You're capable of independent thought, being true to the inner self, and being able to pursue what you truly desire without judgment.

Being self-reliant is crucial to your journey. You'll be able to solve problems and make your own decisions. Your happiness also becomes self-reliant as you become self-actualized, accepted, gather self-compassion, and self-knowledge. Most importantly, it changes your perspective, which changes your direction. You must accept yourself as you are, including your strengths, weaknesses, and passions. You have to be your own best friend. Support yourself and your character strengths, such as courage, curiosity, and kindness. Improve your self-confidence so that you can accept praise when it's due. Inner confidence also requires you to forgo self-judgment and insecurities.

Practice making your own decisions so that you can manage obstacles without requiring help. Decision-making is best practiced, even if you start small. Recognize your dependence on society because the awareness changes your pursuit of their knowledge to inner knowledge. Setting and achieving goals helps you build your self-knowledge. Moreover, work on accepting yourself, including the trust your values, beliefs, and skills provide. Rely on happiness earned internally, and decide who you want to be.

Self-Resilience

Resilience is a character strength we develop. It has nothing to do with the avoidance of stress; it's the ability to remain functional while experiencing stress. It's the capacity to regulate yourself and continue living life while life is crumbling around you. It's your competence to accomplish what you desire, your confidence in your abilities, and your connection to a supportive community that doesn't judge you. It's the moral compass that teaches you right from wrong, the contribution you make to society, and having the ability to cope with stress. It's the emotional control you exude over your battles. It's the way you think about, analyze, and react to stress. Self-resilience requires mental, physical, and emotional elements.

The physical element covers vitality, health, physical strength, and energy, and the mental element contains self-esteem, self-confidence, self-awareness, self-expression, and rationally positive thinking. The emotional aspect is being aware of your emotions to regulate them. You must be mindful, non-judgmental, and flexible enough to cope healthily with the stress you will endure. Self-resilience increases your ability to zoom into the internal feelings you experience, including the dissonance that comes from our actions and values being opposite. You become aware of how your feelings can impact your actions, and you gain a broader understanding of worldly perceptions.

You'll be committed enough to keep persevering, no matter how hard it gets. Practicing self-resilience also improves your emotional well-being and control. Regaining control allows you to manipulate emotions so that you can continue. Self-resilience combined with positive thinking and realism is the key to flexible thinking. Your performance improves during challenges, and you'll even adopt healthier relationships. Flexible thinking, persistence, emotional control, and self-awareness can be practiced. You must remain mindful, recognize that your behaviors are heavily influenced by your thoughts, and be willing to acknowledge stress to cope with it.

Be open to changes, and accept the potential for stress. Changing the way that you cope with stress makes a huge difference. Moreover, work on your self-compassion and empathy. Gratitude is also a precursor for self-resilience, and you can enhance your self-resilience to develop personal skills. Each skill you need for purpose is a double-edged type that's required for your journey and it improves it. Practice self-acceptance, beat procrastination by being willing enough to continue functioning, and open the flood gates of stress rather than hiding from it. Allowing yourself to practice coping with it is the greatest resilience-building tool.

Increase your self-awareness with 10 simple questions. Rate yourself zero to five, with zero indicating that you strongly disagree with the statement and five means that you strongly agree with it.

I trust my choices.

I'm proud of my accomplishments.

I can overcome challenges.

I have people who care about me.

I don't mind criticism.

I respect others and myself.

I enjoy community living.

I know my weaknesses and strengths.

I choose to focus on solutions instead of problems.

I love the life I have.

Total your score, and determine how resilient you are. A score lower than 15 means it needs work, and a score between 16 and 30 indicates average resilience. Scores above 30 are what you want to aim for.

Intuition

Intuition is a key part of being self-reliant, and people have no idea how important gut instinct can be. Stop criticizing the first instinct that springs to mind when you need a solution. Trust it because it comes from the core where your inner strength lies. Intuition allows us to find creative solutions between black and white. Ignoring your intuition is like silencing the brain because those billions of neurons firing are trying to tell you something, even if they were inspired by the gut or heart. Learn to listen to this noise because it has something important to say.

Adopt a curious nature before saying yes or no. Think about the facts behind your instinct, and list the pros and cons before deciding anything. Allow your heart to guide your decision, too. How do these feelings relate to the decision apart from the rational facts you considered? Finally, take a breath, relax, and think about a previous experience where you followed your instinct. Take inspiration from this because chances are that it worked out well. Know that every answer lies within yourself, but you have to trust yourself to hear it.

Responsibility

Taking responsibility for your actions, thoughts, behaviors, and accomplishments is another way to own your purpose and the success of reaching your goals. You can tune into your instincts, self-reliance, and goals as much as you like, but you won't succeed unless you take responsibility for your life. Taking responsibility allows you to know your authentic self and your purpose. You know precisely what you desire, and you consciously choose not to blame other people if you fall short. Moreover, you don't blame yourself, either. Blaming yourself will only deter you from finding a different solution. You'll also learn to be honest with yourself when you're responsible for your life.

You'll become aware of your limits, whether you're too old, financially strapped, or too busy. You can only change what you recognize, after all. Finally, you'll know that you have choices. Taking responsibility for your thoughts, actions, emotions, and words is a start. Your thoughts come from your mind, and accepting this helps your journey. Stop blaming people for your shortfalls, and rather look at what you can improve so that you don't blame yourself, either. Complaining is a subtle form of blame, so stop doing it. Stop taking things personally, and be responsible for manifesting your happiness. Live in the present moment, and set intentions responsibly. Have a vision, and plan to reach it.

Staying positive, and looking for the good in people also helps. Recognize the reason why people do what they do because this helps you release judgment, for them and yourself.

Self-Love

Self-love is the most incredible skill you can develop, and it has nothing to do with society's negative connotations about egotism. Sometimes, it's okay to want to love yourself. Finding the balance between selflessness and selfishness is essential for happiness and the pursuit of a purpose. Erich Fromm wrote *The Art of Loving*, and he understood that love and existence are the same things. Fromm knew that we can't exist without love, and that includes the love for ourselves. Self-love contains four elements, whether it's for ourselves or others.

Care is the first element, which is an active concern for anything and anyone you love, including your authentic self, values, boundaries, and personal growth. We must love life and what grows from it, and we intend to grow our strengths and purpose. Be gentle with yourself and treat yourself with respect to accept who you are. You need concern for your well-being, and the ability to face what doesn't make you happy. It's not always an easy task to find the balance. You must love what you work for and work for what you love.

Responsibility is the second element, and it's the feeling of being able to respond to your desires and needs. You can't possess judgment; you must view responsibility from a caring perspective.

Respect is third, and it means that balanced self-love is achieved by respecting who you truly are and how unique your individualism is. Self-respect is the ability to have concern for your strengths and weakness and to grow what you're authentically capable of being.

Knowledge is fourth, and it's simple; you can't respect your authentic self without knowing yourself thoroughly. Self-responsibility and care would be pointless if you didn't know yourself, and knowledge wouldn't be valuable if you didn't care about it.

Including these four elements in your daily life enhances your self-love without tipping the scales to egotism. Adopt all the skills you need to pursue your purpose, and plan realistic goals to get there. This way, you'll find a good life. However, we're still missing the 'R' of the PERMA pie, which is the next phase.

Chapter 8:

Positive Connections, Healthy Relationships

So far, we've delved directly or indirectly into the 'P,' 'E,' 'M,' and 'A' from the PERMA model in chapter one, which leaves the 'R.' It represents relationships, albeit positive. This chapter teaches you about positive relationships and how to use them to reach your fullest life potential. Some relationships must go, others must be enhanced, and you need a few skills to bundle this neatly.

Positive Psychology and Relationships

Too often, happiness comes with a biased connotation where it's individualized. Each person is supposed to steer a 'happiness' boat to the shore. Even though your happiness is internal, and it relies on everything you choose, do, and perceive, it's also unrealistic if you believe that your boat is alone out there. Instead, think of your happiness as a lighthouse that makes you stand tall while allowing other boats to steer safely to the shore. Human beings remain social, and guiding others with your happiness light maintains this need. We need to bond and depend on other people, so our social connections are intricately intertwined with happiness, and it's a precursor to a meaningful life.

Everyone thrives on the foundation of intimacy, love, mutual respect, and meaningful connections. We yearn for physical and emotional interaction with others. Positive connections aren't only our ability to steer other people's boats to the shore; it's also our boat that's guided gently and merrily by others. Every person is a lighthouse and a boat, including your friends, partner, colleagues, siblings, and parents. We're all floating, waiting for guidance from the lights around us. Knowing that you have this connection already enhances emotional resilience because someone's light will offer support when the sea darkens.

Interestingly, our neural pain centers activate when we're threatened by isolation, which also proves that humans need connections (Pascha, 2019). You've already gathered a plethora of tools in the previous chapters, which allow you to connect with other people. Moreover, you'll know how to be sensitive to their well-being and emotions. Seeking intrinsic happiness while ensuring community contentment offers a deeper intimacy with people. You've learned how to change perspectives without allowing society to cloud your authenticity. Your gratefulness also improves every relationship. Besides, positive thinking generates more positive thinking, making this journey easier by the day.

Positive psychology can take you a long way towards a life worth living in romantic and friendly relationships.

In fact, PP vastly focuses on the connection and interaction between two people because it concludes the happiness pie. Four habits build and maintain strong, positive connections.

Firstly, you need a healthy passion that's void of obsession. Revert to the four elements of love in the previous chapter to understand the foundation of what love means. Obsession is a distorted way of interacting with people. You can't control them, and they can't write your story.

Secondly, healthy connections contain fewer negative emotions. Cultivate positive thoughts and feelings, and work toward removing anything else.

Thirdly, healthy relationships also allow and encourage the necessary time to experience mindful living together. You must mindfully savor every event you share.

Fourthly, good relationships encourage both people to bring out the best in each other. You should be helping each other grow strengths that promote a mutually good life. Each person should also look for the strengths in the other person and avoid looking for every flaw because everyone has them, and looking for them only reveals them.

Every relationship benefits from following the four positive habits mentioned.

Beware the Rocks

What happens when a boat is guided by a fake light? It hits the rocks, and it sinks. Surrounding yourself with toxic people won't help you create healthy connections. It steers your boat to the ocean's bed. Only surround yourself with positive and kind people, and be on the lookout for toxic relationships, which come in any type. Even parents can be toxic, and this is painful to admit. Start with your parents by recognizing frequent toxicity. Parents should never overreact or make a scene when you decide on your future.

It doesn't matter if they want you to be a doctor; it matters if they're bringing you down because you want to be a writer. Some parents go as low as emotional blackmail. Maybe your mom tells you that you don't care about her anymore, and that's why you choose to move across the states. Parents who make frequent demands that don't resonate with your passions are also worrisome, and so are parents who try to control you, especially in adulthood. You don't need parental relationships if they're over-critical, always comparing you to your siblings.

Toxic parents also show no interest in your goals, take no responsibility to apologize when they must, and have no respect for your boundaries. They might blame you, attack your values, and make you feel guilty when blackmail fails. Toxic parents dismiss your feelings, envy you, compete with you, and manipulate you by playing the victim. It's hard to detach physically from your parents, but you can detach emotionally by not reacting to them. Don't pay attention to their behaviors, and stay on your path, whether they like it or not.

Be assertive about your boundaries, and make sure they know what you won't negotiate with. You're allowed to say no when your mom asks daily favors, or your sister can't stop trying to borrow money from you to support her bad habits. Expect retaliation because it will come when you put your foot down. It doesn't make your life any less worth living if they choose not to live in your pocket anymore, either. Allow distance if it's needed. Asserting your boundaries will make them distant anyway.

Friends are another concern because we spend so much time with them. Pay attention to how many times you feel let down by a friend or how often they bring out your worst side. Do you feel pressured to do what you don't want to? Not feeling comfortable with telling your friend important stuff is an instinct telling you not to. An obvious sign is if you're always disagreeing, or maybe the friendship simply feels one-sided. Drama queens and jealousy are red flags, and you can't be positively happy with someone who refuses to improve.

You might not be excited to spend time with them anymore, or respect is nonexistent between you. Even worse, your friend might intentionally and frequently put you down. These signs prevent a happy life, so this relationship needs to be handled. Use your locus of control to decide whether you want this relationship and if you still do, list the advantages and disadvantages of this person to see how you can focus on the positive side to encourage changes. Moreover, space and time are yours.

Take as much as you need to decide if you want this friend in your life, and feel free to take a break from them. Chances are that you'll slowly drift apart when you become positive and happy anyway. Don't blame yourself, take time to gently get over it, and move on by strengthening your connection to friends who treat you with equal appreciation. Toxic friendships don't offer you a lighthouse, no matter how much you care about the person.

Relationships at work can also be toxic. Notice whether you're feeling overwhelmingly stressed during work, whether you sleep enough, and whether your eating habits are any good. Toxic workplaces also cause burnout, frequent illnesses, and chronic fatigue. Are your leadership colleagues narcissistic, always making you agree with their opinions? Your lack of enthusiasm is another sign, and so is a high employee turnover. Pay attention to whether the management team is supportive, or whether they convey poor instructions that cause misunderstandings.

Workplaces filled with cliques, rumors, and gossip are also toxic. You could find colleagues who feel the same and create a support network where you watch each other's backs. Participating in stress-reducing activities after work also helps, but avoid negative habits. Design lists that keep you busy at work, journal everything you do and how it makes you feel, and begin the exit strategy. The best chance you have of a good life is to get out of a workplace that doesn't appreciate you. Look for a better opportunity before exiting.

Any relationship can be toxic, and you need to scan your circle for the warning signs. People who always worry are living a mentally unhealthy diet of negativity, which will become yours. Anyone who acts controlling should also go and stay away from people who live in the default mode of fear, anxiety, and negative emotions. The default position is the negativity bias, so steer clear of these people because it's contagious. People who exude weird secrecy are also concerning because they don't love themselves enough to show their authentic selves.

Avoid people who always find drama. Some people look for it, and they become magnets. Their drama becomes yours. Be careful of people who complain about everything, even the mailman who forgot to take their mail after they raised their signal flag. People who can't handle constructive criticism are also worrisome, and you can't flourish with people who take compliments out of context. Watch for anyone afraid of moving out of their comfort zones because they'll keep you in yours.

Toxic people are famous for being underachievers because they can't overcome procrastination and they'll never pursue anything concrete, meaning that they won't encourage you to pursue your dreams. Watch for double standard talking if someone uses the word 'but' in every compliment, too. "You look nice, but your hair's messy." Excitement is also not part of their intentions for the future. You might feel like they're draining your positive energy, and they'll always look for the negative, even with good news. You have two options. You can let go of these people entirely or stop feeding their vampire tendencies.

Ignore their negative propaganda, and smile big when they say something stupid. Responding allows them to fight back negatively, but ignoring them and showing kindness is the way you end the conversation or change the topic. You certainly don't need to defend yourself or your choices. Carry on with your journey, and you'll remain happy among new, positive people as long as you never intentionally hurt someone, even the toxic clowns. Let them go, or put an end to the influence they have over you.

Building Deep Connections

You might've realized that you have a few diamonds among the rough toxins, and if not, work on building new, positive relationships. If you have a few good relationships, work on them by adopting three attitudes.

Healthy Problem-Solving

Being able to solve a problem the right way deepens the bond, and it prevents lingering resentment. The reason why this is essential in relationships is that everyone views things differently. No two people think alike, even if they love each other. Problems also aren't only extreme cases like divorce or the end of a friendship. Not agreeing on the lunch spot, the color of the nursery or the movie can be problems. A problem is defined, in this case, as two people who struggle to agree on something, big or small.

The doubt in your mind needs a solution so that you can agree. Problems also occur because one person doesn't understand the other person's view, or they don't know how to respond to it. Problems have two common facets: goals and challenges. What is the challenge you face in this disagreement? What is the common goal you want to achieve? Those are the two things that you need to answer to prevent a problem from destroying a relationship, but use the resolution steps to help.

Step one is to mutually recognize and define the issue. Discuss what defines the disagreement for both of you.

Step two is to structure the issue. This requires analyzing it from both perspectives. How does the problem make you feel, and what facts support your perspective? Allow your friend or partner to provide their structure.

Step three is when you have clarity on the definition and structure, and both of you have a good understanding of how the other person feels. Now, choose three solutions you can think of, and allow them to do the same.

Step four is where you need to decide on a solution between six options. You must both give reasons why you chose these options so you're on the same level.

Step five is where you implement the change to resolve the disagreement. Both parties must accept the decided solution, and that means no take-backs.

Step six is where you monitor how the solution is making both parties feel, how it improves mutual happiness, and where you discuss subjective feedback with each other. Explain how this solution is or isn't working for you, and perhaps, you can start at step one again.

Generosity

Generosity is the act of selflessness toward others. It's when you're kind, understanding, and prepared to share valuable time, items, and knowledge with people. Being generous to another person promotes closeness between you. The reason you feel closer to them is that generosity encourages you to understand their perspective positively. It creates a sense of interconnectedness and community. The root of generosity can also be linked to our biology. We survive better through a collective community, and generosity is one of the methods we use to enforce it. Generosity activates the same neural pathways as sex and food according to The Greater Good Science Center (Allen, 2018).

Generosity makes you more thoughtful, compassionate, and grateful. People are more likely to reciprocate the way you treat them, and being prepared to share your best self is the height of deeper connections. Start this improvement by considering its benefits on your social life, and you'll already be working on it when you hone your gratitude skills. You don't have to start big. Start small by doing something meaningful for someone. Consider the person's needs and desires, and spend time with them if this is what suits their needs best. Offer them help when they need to finish a project for work.

The important thing is that you offer generosity first. Don't wait for it to happen to you before you reciprocate. You might've been famous for not appreciating generosity, so people don't bother. And when someone offers generosity in return, appreciate it wholeheartedly. You can also meet new people by donating a small amount of money to a charity that grabs your heart. Show friends that you believe in them, and support their efforts and dreams. Know that not everyone will return your generosity.

Offer your time to help people in need, and have meaningful conversations. Sometimes, the best thing you can offer is time, and having a deep conversation with someone can be an act of kindness toward them. Show real interest in their stories. Most importantly, be generous enough to your positive social network to share your dreams and hopes with them. This is another priceless thing you can give them because it lets them know that they're part of your inner circle.

Compassion

Whether you're self-compassionate, or you want to deepen your connection with someone else, compassion is a skill you can't ignore. Compassion is a route to happiness in PP. It's a mental state used to respond to people's suffering, including yours. Your compassion should motivate people's behaviors to relieve their suffering. The best and most consistent way you can adopt compassion for yourself and others to strengthen relationships is to practice compassion meditation. This form of meditation increases your interconnectedness and understanding of suffering in yourself and others (Ribiero, 2019).

Moreover, it's a way we can learn altruism toward the needs of other people, and our minds benefit from the positive intentions we wish upon someone else by experiencing them first. Compassion helps us cope with insecurities and fears, and it calms the mind. There's even a therapy called compassion-focused therapy (CFT) designed around it. Improved well-being is the first benefit, but it also elevates your emotional intelligence, which is required for deeper connections with friends and family. Compassion meditation also cultivates empathy, benevolence, and love.

There are only two steps to practice compassion meditation.

Step one is where you must intend to expect nothing. Get comfortable, and set your mind to zero recipient expectations. You may set intentions to give compassion, but expect nothing in return. Take 60 seconds to focus on improving your compassion toward others unconditionally. Close your eyes, or keep them open. This isn't a strictly disciplined meditation. Your intentions are the most vital part of it.

Step two requires systematic visualization. Start with the person you feel closest to before moving on to the relationship that requires some work if you're focused on compassion for others. Otherwise, start with your smallest problem and work toward the biggest one in your visualization. Now, practice sending and receiving compassion with this person by imagining a scenario where you say something kind when they feel down, and imagine them thanking you, which shows appreciation and is already a return of compassion.

Go through your systematic list, and send and receive with each person. You can practice these steps informally or formally. Use them when you feel overwhelmed by someone, and visualize your compassion before offering it. You can also use the informal breathing method when you see someone suffering. Focus mindfully on breathing compassion in and allowing the suffering to leave your mind when you breathe out. Approach the person, and teach them to do the same.

Improving your relationships by removing the wrong people and deepening your connection with the right people concludes the PERMA pie of a good life. The final stage is where you'll start implementing everything you've learned.

Chapter 9:

Moving Forward and Taking Matters Into Your Own Hands

You've learned about the foundational changes you need to make. These new habits make you think and behave more positively, and you'll be set for a good, meaningful life. It's time to recap the main points so that you can apply them to your life and become autonomous in your journey, leaping into the exploration and potential of a new future.

Fordyce's Fundamentals

Psychologist Michael Fordyce is a name we haven't explored here, but he also researched positive psychology, and he realized that there are 14 fundamentals we need in our lives to become positive thinkers and enjoy each day (Chowdhury, 2019e). The interventions you've learned about and the changes you'll implement are in response to his fundamentals. We'll bundle them together to understand how you'll apply them better.

The first fundamental is that we must become more active and stay busy. You can't benefit from anything in life unless you become proactively involved. This fundamental touches on a few exercises and changes you learned about. It starts with getting active enough to strengthen your core, which is the very place your gut instincts manifest. It's the same place our physical power hails from, and applying simple workouts can make the center of your physical strength stronger so that you can face the changes with finesse and certainty.

Sign up with a personal trainer who can teach you how to strengthen this area. Yoga is also known to work on the core muscles, and better posture brings benefits, too. Pursuing your goals also touches this fundamental because you need to actively make changes, even if it starts in your mind and on paper first. The "just do it" philosophy encourages you to just start your goals, and you'll feel the momentous motivation that comes from proactively starting your journey.

The second fundamental is that we must spend more time in our social life. Socializing for a positive life is done by removing the people who take you under and replacing them with people who push you forward in your journey. They should encourage and support you, especially when it comes to family and friends. Go out there, and put yourself into positions that further enhance your positivity and better life by volunteering and meeting like-minded people instead. Some amazing benefits come from two people appreciating each other, enjoying the experience together, and expressing optimism and joy toward each other.

The third fundamental is to be productive at work. Productivity and creativity are enhanced with a few simple changes, and of course, you aim to reach the flow state if you love your work. Loving your work is the first step, and removing yourself from a toxic workplace is the second step, but reaching the state of flow in your work will raise your performance to new heights. You'll be soaring through each task, instead of dragging your feet. You also know how to look for the positive edge in everything you do, so challenges won't seem as insurmountable anymore. Moreover, mistakes are simply a part of the journey, even at work. Setting SMART goals, taking responsibility for your life, and adopting the habit of positive exploration are merely a few ways you assert this fundamentality.

The fourth fundamental is to be more organized in your life. Chaos breeds misery, and it certainly doesn't help you in your journey of positivity and happiness. Setting goals that align with your purpose, and doing it in a manner that improves your chance of success already organizes your life so that you know where you're headed. Creative visualization and visualizing your best self provide mental clarity on what needs to be done, and connecting the body and mind allows them to work in sync. The skills required to attend to your calling also offer organization because you need to take responsibility for the good and bad. It allows you to regain your locus of control, and your journey becomes easier once you have control again.

The fifth fundamental is to reduce negative contemplations and worry in your life. Most of what you've learned targets this fundamental, but there are a few that stand out. Learning to combine optimism and realism sets the stage for positive thinking. There's science behind optimism and how certain areas in the brain activate, leading to positive emotions. You have the mechanics, and now you know how to trick the brain into switching this process on.

Optimism allows you to challenge your thoughts on the same playing field, and it comes with an added benefit of hope. Hope remains an incredible emotion, and it allows you to face worries with less fear. You also know how to affirm your journey and how meditation can release negative emotions. Gratitude yoga and meditation also provide relief from anxious emotions. Moreover, learned helplessness is diminished by learning optimism, rewiring your brain, and turning your inner critic into your friend.

The sixth fundamental is to have fewer societal expectations and to rely on your realistic standards instead. Simply being aware of how society has influenced you from childhood to the expectations that you must look this way, act that way, and think like a drone is a start. Rewiring your thoughts in chapter two helps you to realize where your expectations come from and how you can change them. You must face your inner critics and silence them if they don't improve your journey. You know how to manage self-doubt and enhance your authentic inner self to be confident enough to pursue your dreams.

The seventh fundamental is to practice optimism through positive thinking and rationality. Optimism requires balance, and you can't wear rose-colored glasses because this won't help you to experience every aspect of life. Even worse, it will make you experience dreadful emotions when you make mistakes because you never expected them. You're in charge of your positive thoughts and emotions, but life always brings challenges to your journey. How you deal with them is what makes the difference. Optimism is a great trait that offers many health benefits, but adding reason to it is how you prevent negative landslides when life chooses to throw a lemon at you.

The eighth fundamental is to be mindful of the present moment and to increase your focus because the present is the only reality that exists at any given time. Living in the past is a recipe for emotional distress, and living in the future ignites anxiety and fear. You can plan for the future with past experience, but you have to use the passions in your present moment to combine happiness and purpose. Grounding yourself in the present moment where you can connect the past, present, and future is easily achieved with meditation and mindfulness. Everything you do and everything you experience needs to be in the present moment. The past should only serve as inspiration, and the future is a goal, but the present is where joy, happiness, hope, and an appreciation for life exist.

The ninth fundamental is to develop and maintain a healthy personality, which is best done by focusing on your character strengths to improve them for better results in the future. The flow state can help you do this if you're focusing on activities that you excel with. Just remember that they also need to provide a challenge, or you won't be improving your character traits. Respecting your authentic self, and learning about positive self-love also enhances your healthy personality, and so does the practice of gratitude.

Knowing what you've already achieved and how you make other people feel can boost your self-worth. Apply the gratitude challenge so that you can adopt self-appreciation because you need to accept your true self to possess a healthy personality. Make positive changes in your life, such as gratitude journaling, becoming self-reliant, and increasing your emotional resilience because nothing can stand in your way if you do.

The tenth fundamental is to become more empathetic to yourself and others. Everyone experiences suffering at some point in their lives, whether it's losing a job or breaking up with their girlfriend. Teaching yourself to become compassionate is how you show people empathy, and these are the same people that join your journey to positivity and a good life. Volunteer work is another practice in which you exercise your empathy, and you can achieve this fundamental of happiness by donating your valuable time and effort to charities.

You might even find your meaning by signing up for an organization that feeds the hungry and tries to end the suffering of others. Self-compassion teaches you to be empathetic with your emotions because it doesn't matter how much control you gain over them; life still has a way of shaking you down with mistakes and failures. Empathy also improves relationships, giving you the community aspect required to lead a life worth living.

The eleventh fundamental is to be your authentic self, or you won't be happy or positive. Authenticity allows us to follow our dreams with our passions and purpose. You're as uniquely individual as the next person, and your values are no less meaningful than theirs. You can't find happiness by pursuing other people's dreams and living by their standards. Welcome your true self so that you can flourish in this journey. Besides, people tend to distance themselves from unauthentic friends, so you won't be doing your community any favors by being fake. Learn to listen to your gut instinct because it's often your true self speaking from your heart and core.

The flow state also teaches you how to allow the inner self to come to the spotlight by transcending into a deeper mindset where the subconscious mind experiences the external world. Your boss will appreciate you more for being authentic, and if they don't, it's time to look elsewhere for what makes you happy enough to perform better. All of your relationships will enhance when you're true to yourself, and your happiness and motivation become intrinsic when they line themselves with what truly matters to you.

The twelfth fundamental is to replace negative thoughts with positive thinking, which is done the moment you challenge your thoughts. You can reconstruct failure when you understand that thoughts are merely opinions instigated by the inner critic, whichever one takes center stage. Journaling gives these thoughts a voice, which sometimes silences them once they have the proper attention. Don't stop your musical role exercise in chapter three, either. It allows you to step out of your mind, distancing yourself from the opinions flowing through your mind and giving you the space to rethink them.

Understanding how these thoughts are processed, and how you can lay new pathways in the brain will take their power away. It only requires patience and practice to rewire the network between your prefrontal cortex and the nucleus accumbens. Your brain will retaliate at first, but time will change this, and emotions won't influence your logical thoughts anymore. You'll break through the cognitive distortions and inhibitions with the persistent practice of your new habits.

The thirteenth fundamental is to value close relationships enough to deepen the connection. Learning how to disagree amicably and resolve issues with maturity allows you the benefit of garnering closer relationships. You learn to see other people's perspectives without bending your boundaries unless you want to compromise a little. Moreover, use the empathetic, compassionate, and generous traits you've learned about to show the person how much you love or appreciate them. Love is also not a misguided emotion anymore now that you understand the four elements of it.

Care, responsibility, respect, and knowledge pave the way to better relationships with deserving people who aren't toxic. Relationships become positive with simple changes, and you can flourish in the community that pushes you ahead of your dreams. Everyone needs a positive connection with someone to prevent the survival instinct from derailing their happiness, and oxytocin is the most powerful depressant of the fight or flight response.

The fourteenth and final fundamental of positively living a worthy life is to think about enhancing your happiness. Creative visualization is a powerful tool to ensure that you're focused on who you want to be, your best self, and how you want to make the changes. Combine the facets to reach a flow state with your creative visualization, and your subconscious mind can process the experience when you get lost in the moment. Visualize everything you want and how it makes you feel, and the level of engagement helps the subconscious mind store the information for motivation. Give your inner self genuine sensory experiences by allowing activities you love to challenge you enough to reach the flow state.

A Final Encouragement

Everything you need is neatly laid out for you, and the evidence doesn't lie. Use your strategies to create the 14 fundamentals of a good and positive life, and you'll also be covering every piece of Seligman's PERMA model. Indulge in the positive emotions required for the 'P' by practicing optimism, gratitude, compassion, and intrinsic happiness. Continue experiencing everything in the present moment to benefit from your positive mindset. The 'E' for engagement is practiced by engaging with all five of your senses in every experience. It can also be reached in the flow state once you master it, allowing you to engage fully at your whim.

The 'R' for relationships, albeit positive, is also covered when you build a community of like-minded people to connect with deeply. You also know what your options are with the toxic people who won't help your new life. The 'M' for meaning is extensively explored to help you find your calling. Everyone needs meaning in life, and your purpose is a few steps away if you discover it and set goals to pursue it the right way. The 'A' for accomplishment will come to you as soon as you review your progress on this journey. You'll learn to acknowledge the achievements you make, and you know how to appreciate yourself enough to make the subconscious mind store the information.

Your new life is waiting with both models explored and explained comprehensively. Use the human mind to write the story you deserve because that's it's purpose. It's where rationality, passion, ambitions, character traits, and control lies. You simply need to take control of it, so never stop living in the present moment. Stop thinking too hard about the future or past because they can only inspire you. They don't make up your present reality, and they can't make you happy right now. Move forward on your journey by practicing self-love, compassion, gratitude, and positive thinking. Keep making an effort to understand your emotions because that's key to understanding the human mind.

Strive to keep evolving into a better person, and remember that none of your life is set in stone. You can decide to make a radical change to improve and grow at any moment. Keep journaling your progress and exploring your inner self. We're constantly changing, and our mind and being are profoundly capable of accepting the fact that we won't always understand why and how we function completely, but it's a good goal to keep striving for. Remember that failure is also merely an opportunity to learn and grow, and most importantly, enjoy every moment of your journey.

Conclusion

The human mind is truly a fascinating organ with powers beyond understanding entirely. It can either be hostile and negative due to conditioning and primal instincts, or it can use these same aspects to improve your life. Negativity only allows the mind to resemble a saboteur, but positivity turns it into the most powerful friend you'll ever control. The sabotaging consequences were the reason you needed this book. Negativity has likely consumed your life and happiness to a point where you realized that changes were needed.

Negativity is so automatic that it impacts every part of your life. It ruins relationships, and it prevents you from having the supportive community you need to flourish. You can't spread your wings when these thoughts and emotions pop into your mind as though it's playing ping pong with your future. Moreover, it hurts you further when your negative mindset removes people you might truly love. The only people who tend to stick around aren't cheering for you. Chances are that they're manipulating you or taking advantage of your need for acceptance and approval.

Society has a strange way of depicting our beliefs and expectations, always steering us away from happiness. It gets worse at work when your performance and happiness dissipate over time. Your career doesn't make you feel happy, and neither does the negative feelings surrounding it. It's hard to admit, but some people despise their jobs. We can't help it if we don't find satisfaction in what we do. However, resentment is only a stew of negative emotions that make your life even harder. Sometimes, you wonder what it is that you resent. It's okay to admit that you resent your life.

You find yourself reaching for dreams, whether they belong to you or not. Unfortunately, you fall short of achieving them because your motivation flies out of the window. You're simmering in negative thoughts and feelings that only amplify with every missed opportunity and failed goal. Do you ever ask yourself what the meaning of your life is? This is another consequence of negativity and unhappiness. The other side of the human mind is where your best friend lives. This friend can help you design a life that promotes well-being, happiness, and success. Neuroscience proved that it's there. It's waiting for activation and reconnection to the logical and positive sides of the brain.

Being positive changes everything in your life. Your journey becomes more pleasant, and your relationships thrive. Your career and performance reach opportunistic levels, and your intrinsic motivation drives the train straight to your desired life. You can become your best self, and the answer lies within your mind. Knowing what your purpose in this life is will allow the friendly part of your mind to take action. You know where your expectations come from now, and you understand how they impact your self-perception, self-esteem, and positivity. If only you had this information sooner so that you could use science and the positive side of psychology to awaken the friendly mind.

It's time to face the saboteur and take its power away. You won't drown in expectations and learned helplessness by applying the models of positive psychology, and you get a showdown with those inner critics that make you feel worse. Removing the cognitive inhibitions pushes you closer to finding your fullest potential in everything you do and experience. The saboteur's loop habits will change when you practice the habits laid out in this book. Some simple exercises help you do that, and you don't need to fear mistakes and failure anymore. You can finally adopt realistic optimism that doesn't cloud your judgment or expectations, and you know that it's best to challenge negative thoughts head-on.

Meditation and scientifically-proven practices bring you closer to a happy and fulfilling life by reconnecting the mind and body so that you can behave positively, too. Who knew that laughing was such an incredible experience? Mindfulness also allows you to reconnect your mind and body so that you regain control over the powerful organ that designs your future. You know how to experience everything in the only time that matters, and your senses help you trick the structure of your brain to think more effectively. Gratitude has made you see life from a different angle now and applying it benefits you neurologically and emotionally. It also benefits every relationship you have, including the one you adopt with your inner self.

Even better, you can enter a state of mind that breaks down any obstacles in your path, and you need to love the activity to achieve it, so there's joy in every little moment. Using transcendence opens your world to opportunities that were never possible, and it challenges you to explore them. This fills your life with new skills and positive emotions. Three secrets help you find this state of mind, and once there, you'll never regret practicing it. The flow state can even guide you through your purpose, and a life with purpose is certainly a life worth living.

You know how to reach for goals that resonate with everything you believe in, and your resilience, responsibility, and reliance among other skills will ensure your success. Relationships will also flourish now that you can remove the thorns on your rosebush. Learning how to bond deeper is how you surround yourself with cheerleaders because that's the type of community and relationships you need to guarantee a good life. Everything you need is within your control now. Every trick, biological hack, and simple practice is as far away as you choose. Implement what you've learned, and allow yourself to be showered in possibilities that were once clouded by a negative saboteur.

References

Ackerman, C. (2019, July 10). *What is positive psychology & why is it important?* Positive Psychology. https://positivepsychology.com/what-is-positive-psychology-definition/

Allen, S. (2018). *The science of generosity.* In Berkeley. https://ggsc.berkeley.edu/images/uploads/GGSC-JTF_White_Paper-Generosity-FINAL.pdf

Allen, S. (2019). *Positive neuroscience.* In Berkeley. https://ggsc.berkeley.edu/images/uploads/White_Paper_Positive_Neuroscience_FINAL.pdf

Baumeister, R. F., Vohs, K. D., Aaker, J. L., & Garbinsky, E. N. (2013). Some key differences between a happy life and a meaningful life. *The Journal of Positive Psychology*, 8(6), 505–516. https://doi.org/10.1080/17439760.2013.830764

Becker, J. (2011). *10 little ways to become more generous.* Becoming Minimalist. https://www.becomingminimalist.com/10-simple-ways-to-become-a-more-generous-person/

Bhandari, N. (2019, September 26). *Inescapable importance of acceptance.* Times of India Blog. https://timesofindia.indiatimes.com/readersblo

g/soulful-connect/inescapable-importance-of-acceptance-5885/

Blundell, A. (2016, August 30). *Setting expectations too high - is this behind your low moods and stress?* Harley TherapyTM Blog. https://www.harleytherapy.co.uk/counselling/setting-expectations.htm#:~:text=High%20expectations%20often%20come%20connected

Brenner, A. (2016). *The benefits of creative visualization.* Psychology Today. https://www.psychologytoday.com/us/blog/in-flux/201606/the-benefits-creative-visualization

Campbell, P. (2019, February 5). *Why hope matters.* Psychology Today. https://www.psychologytoday.com/us/blog/imperfect-spirituality/201902/why-hope-matters

Carpenter, D. (2007, February 22). *Visualizing happiness.* Positive Psychology News. https://positivepsychologynews.com/news/derrick-carpenter/20070222123

Changing Minds. (n.d.-a). *Positive emotions.* Changing Minds. http://changingminds.org/explanations/emotions/positive_emotions.htm#:~:text=Positive%20emotion%20may%20be%20considered

Cherry, K., & Lechman, S. (2019). *The optimism bias: Are you too optimistic for your own good?* Verywell Mind.

https://www.verywellmind.com/what-is-the-optimism-bias-2795031

Cherry, K., & Snyder, C. (2011, March 2). *"Flow" can help you achieve goals*. Verywell Mind. https://www.verywellmind.com/what-is-flow-2794768

Cherry, K., & Swaim, E. (2019). *Why our brains are hardwired to focus on the negative*. Verywell Mind. https://www.verywellmind.com/negative-bias-4589618

Chong, C. (2017, March 22). *Signs of low self-esteem and the root causes you might not know*. Lifehack. https://www.lifehack.org/565816/low-self-esteem

Chowdhury, Madhuleena R. (2019a, January 22). *What is emotional resilience and how to build it? (+Training exercises)*. Positive Psychology. https://positivepsychology.com/emotional-resilience/

Chowdhury, Madhuleena R. (2019b, April 9). *Guided gratitude meditation scripts & mantras (+gratitude yoga)*. Positive Psychology. https://positivepsychology.com/guided-gratitude-meditation/

Chowdhury, Madhuleena R. (2019c, April 9). *The neuroscience of gratitude and how it affects anxiety & grief*. Positive Psychology. https://positivepsychology.com/neuroscience-of-gratitude/

Chowdhury, Madhuleena R. (2019d, June 19). *5 health benefits of daily meditation according to science.* Positive Psychology. https://positivepsychology.com/benefits-of-meditation/

Chowdhury, Madhuleena R. (2019e, July 10). *19 best positive psychology interventions + how to apply them.* Positive Psychology. https://positivepsychology.com/positive-psychology-interventions/

Chowdhury, Mahuleena R. (2020, January 9). *11 optimism tools, examples and exercises to help improve your outlook.* Positive Psychology. https://positivepsychology.com/optimism-tools-exercises-examples/

Cohen, A. (2011, January 12). *Expansive posture: When you've got it, flaunt it!* Positive Psychology News. https://positivepsychologynews.com/news/aren-cohen/2011011216017#:~:text=Good%20posture%20connotes%20confidence%2C%20leadership%20and%20power.&text=When%20a%20person%20sits%20or

Craig, H. (2019, March 3). The research on gratitude and its link with love and happiness. Positive Psychology. https://positivepsychology.com/gratitude-research/

Dabell, J. (2018, May 1). *The 7 cs of resilience*. John Dabell. https://johndabell.com/2018/05/01/the-7-cs-of-resilience/

Daws, M. (2014, November 12). *When you start to accept things you can't control in life, these 10 amazing things will happen*. Lifehack. https://www.lifehack.org/articles/communication/10-things-that-will-happen-when-you-start-accept-change-your-life.html

Dipirro, D. (2010). *6 ideas for bringing more laughter into your life*. Positively Present. https://www.positivelypresent.com/2010/04/laughter.html

Djordjevic, M. (2020, May 2). 17 undeniable negative news statistics you need to know. Letterly.ly. 17 Undeniable Negative News Statistics You Need To Know (letter.ly)

Fabrega, M. (2015, March 31). *17 ways to be kind to yourself*. Daring to Live Fully. https://daringtolivefully.com/how-to-be-kind-to-yourself

Firefly. (2017, December 18). *Flow: The secret to positive attitude*. SOVA. https://sova.pitt.edu/be-positive-flow-the-secret-to-happiness

Firestone, L. (2014, June 13). *The benefits of generosity*. HuffPost. https://www.huffpost.com/entry/the-benefits-of-generosit_b_5448218?guccounter=1

Fox, G. R., Kaplan, J., Damasio, H., & Damasio, A. (2015). Neural correlates of gratitude. *Frontiers in Psychology*, 6. https://doi.org/10.3389/fpsyg.2015.01491

Fromm, E. (1957). *The art of loving*. Filosofia Esoterica. http://www.filosofiaesoterica.com/wp-content/uploads/2017/01/Erich-Fromm_The-Art-Of-Loving.pdf

Gosselin, S. H. (2020, May 12). *The burden of being ungrateful*. Boundless. https://www.boundless.org/faith/the-burden-of-being-ungrateful/

Greenberg, S. (n.d.). *Nine reasons to embrace failure - motivation*. Boxing Scene. https://www.boxingscene.com/motivation/2603.php#:~:text=Failure%20makes%20us%20stronger.

Guerrera, J. (2017, August 24). *Why you need to fail to succeed*. Medium. https://livingforimprovement.com/why-you-need-to-fail-to-succeed-1594f91decc2

Hani, J. (2017, August 8). *The neuroscience of behavior change*. Medium; Health Transformer. https://healthtransformer.co/the-neuroscience-of-behavior-change-bcb567fa83c1

Heinrich, S. (2020, April 10). *Healthy relationship and positive psychology*. Clarity Clinic. https://claritychi.com/relationship-positivepsychology/#:~:text=Positive%20psychology%20within%20a%20relationship

Hope Grows Editor. (2018, December 22). *Why is hope so important? | understand the deeper meaning of hope.* Hope Grows. https://hopegrows.net/news/why-is-hope-so-important#:~:text=To%20have%20hope%20is%20to

Houston, E. (2019a, April 9). *How to express gratitude to others (19 ideas + gifts & challenges).* Positive Psychology. https://positivepsychology.com/how-to-express-gratitude/

Houston, E. (2019b, June 19). *What is goal setting and how to do it well.* Positive Psychology. https://positivepsychology.com/goal-setting/

Hughes, C. (2019, March 8). *The neuroscience secrets for positive change that stick.* Forbes. https://www.forbes.com/sites/ellevate/2019/03/08/the-neuroscience-secrets-for-positive-change-that-stick/?sh=182005f86305

Hurst, K. (2014, September 19). *Creative visualization: 6 steps to begin using creative visualization.* The Law of Attraction. https://www.thelawofattraction.com/6-steps-to-begin-using-creative-visualization/

In-Between. (2019a, May 29). *Making "just do it" your life philosophy.* In-Between.

https://okaytobeinbetween.com/2019/05/29/just-do-it-life-philosophy/

James, M. (2015, May 17). *6 signs that fear is holding you back*. Psychology Today. https://www.psychologytoday.com/us/blog/focus-forgiveness/201505/6-signs-fear-is-holding-you-back

Joseph, F. (2018, September 22). *Flow benefits: What's in it for you? - get better results faster*. Leadership & Flow. https://flowleadership.org/flow-benefits/#:~:text=Researchers%20have%20found%20that%20one

Kelly, A. (2019, May 29). *Are you self-critical?* Psychology Today. https://www.psychologytoday.com/intl/blog/all-about-attitude/201905/are-you-self-critical

Kessel, A. (2011, June 15). *Find your calling: 5 steps to identify your purpose*. Tiny Buddha. https://tinybuddha.com/blog/find-your-calling-5-steps-to-identify-your-purpose/

Kids Help Phone. (n.d.-b). *Friends forever? How to deal with a toxic friendship*. Kids Help Phone. https://kidshelpphone.ca/get-info/friends-forever-how-deal-toxic-friendship/

Klemp, N. (2019, August 7). *The neuroscience of breaking out of negative thinking (and how to do it in under 30 seconds)*. Inc. https://www.inc.com/nate-klemp/try-this-neuroscience-based-technique-to-shift-your-mindset-from-negative-to-positive-in-30-seconds.html

Lachmann, S. (2013). *10 sources of low self-esteem.* Psychology Today. https://www.psychologytoday.com/us/blog/me-we/201312/10-sources-low-self-esteem

LaMeaux, E. C. (2019). *7 health benefits of laughter.* Gaiam. https://www.gaiam.com/blogs/discover/7-health-benefits-of-laughter

Lancer, D. (2018, August 31). *12 clues a relationship with a parent is toxic.* Psychology Today. https://www.psychologytoday.com/za/blog/toxic-relationships/201808/12-clues-relationship-parent-is-toxic

Leahy, R. (2019, September 10). *How to defeat your self-criticism.* Psychology Today. https://www.psychologytoday.com/us/blog/anxiety-files/201909/how-defeat-your-self-criticism

Legg, L. (n.d.). *Why fear limits your life potential.* Trans4mind. https://trans4mind.com/counterpoint/index-happiness-wellbeing/legg6.html

Live Your True Story. (2020, October 15). *What it means to take responsibility. 7 essential requirements.* Live Your True Story. https://www.liveyourtruestory.com/take-responsibility-performance/

Locke, R. (2015, July 12). *15 signs of negative people.* Lifehack. https://www.lifehack.org/293018/15-signs-negative-people

Lonczak, H. S. (2020, July 8). *Humor in psychology: Coping and laughing your woes away.* Positive Psychology. https://positivepsychology.com/humor-psychology/

Maiolino, N. B., & Kuiper, N. A. (2014). Integrating humor and positive psychology approaches to psychological well-being. *Europe's Journal of Psychology,* 10(3), 557–570. https://doi.org/10.5964/ejop.v10i3.753

Marais, D. (2018, March 4). *9 ways to take responsibility for your life.* Thrive Global. https://thriveglobal.com/stories/9-ways-to-take-responsibility-for-your-life/

Mayo Clinic Staff. (2016). *Stress relief from laughter? It's no joke.* Mayo Clinic. https://www.mayoclinic.org/healthy-lifestyle/stress-management/in-depth/stress-relief/art-20044456

Mikva, R. S. (2019, February 6). *Optimism vs. hope – and other differences that matter.* Vocation Matters. https://vocationmatters.org/2019/02/06/optimism-vs-hope/#:~:text=Optimism%20is%20the%20belief%20that

Miller, Kelly. (2019, August 22). *7 gratitude questionnaires and scales that scientists use.* Positive Psychology. https://positivepsychology.com/measure-gratitude-questionnaires-scales/

Miller, Kori. (2019a, July 2). *14 health benefits of practicing gratitude according to science.* Positive Psychology. https://positivepsychology.com/benefits-of-gratitude/

Miller, Kori. (2019b, August 22). *What is meditation therapy and what are the benefits?* Positive Psychology. https://positivepsychology.com/meditation-therapy/

Minsky, B. (2018, October 22). *How to overcome low self-esteem and negativity.* Thrive Global. https://thriveglobal.com/stories/how-to-overcome-low-self-esteem-and-negativity/

Moore, C. (2019a, March 4). *Positive daily affirmations: Is there science behind it?* Positive Psychology. https://positivepsychology.com/daily-affirmations/

Moore, C. (2019b, April 15). *What is self-reliance and how to develop it?* Positive Psychology. https://positivepsychology.com/self-reliance/

Moore, C. (2019c, June 27). *Learned optimism: Is Martin Seligman's glass half full?* Positive Psychology. https://positivepsychology.com/learned-optimism/

Moore, C. (2019d, July 12). *What is eudaimonia? Aristotle and eudaimonic well-being.* Positive Psychology. https://positivepsychology.com/eudaimonia/

Muguku, D. (2017, February 21). *The positive side of fear & 15 benefits of fear.* ThriveYard. https://www.thriveyard.com/the-positive-side-of-fear-15-benefits-of-fear/#:~:text=At%20the%20basic%20level%20fear

Murphy, A. (2020, January 21). *11 ways to overcome low self esteem.* Declutter The Mind. https://declutterthemind.com/blog/how-to-overcome-low-self-esteem/

Nortje, A. (2020, May 20). *The gratitude journal: Prompts, pdfs and worksheets.* Positive Psychology. https://positivepsychology.com/gratitude-journal-pdf/

O'Brien, M. (2018, August 20). *4 keys to overcoming negative thinking for good.* Mrs. Mindfulness. https://mrsmindfulness.com/the-four-keys-to-overcoming-negative-thinkingfor-good/

Oppland, M. (2017, April 28). *13 most popular gratitude exercises & activities [2019 update].* Positive Psychology. https://positivepsychology.com/gratitude-exercises/

Oppland, M. (2019, July 16). *8 ways to create flow according to Mihaly Csikszentmihalyi [+TED talk].* Positive Psychology.

https://positivepsychology.com/mihaly-csikszentmihalyi-father-of-flow/

Panugan, J. (2020, July 2). *Let go of negative people*. Medium. https://jadepanugan.medium.com/let-go-of-negative-people-27968e6e6a71

Parker, H. (2020, February 29). *Facing your inner critic*. Psychology Today. https://www.psychologytoday.com/us/blog/your-future-self/202002/facing-your-inner-critic

Pascha, M. (2019, July 3). *The PERMA model: Your scientific theory of happiness*. Positive Psychology. https://positivepsychology.com/perma-model/

Pincott, J. E. (2019). *Silencing your inner critic*. Psychology Today. https://www.psychologytoday.com/us/articles/201903/silencing-your-inner-critic

Pogosyan, M. (2018, February 2). *Be kind to yourself*. Psychology Today. https://www.psychologytoday.com/us/blog/between-cultures/201802/be-kind-yourself

Positive Psychlopedia. (2015, February 2). *What is optimism?* The Positive Psychlopedia. https://positivepsychlopedia.com/year-of-happy/what-is-optimism/

Posture, G. (2017, May 11). *First impressions: The psychology of good posture*. Medium. https://medium.com/@goodposturecom/first-impressions-the-psychology-of-good-posture-bd180bcb2c10

Prevost, S. (2012, December 17). *8 signs you're a control freak*. Inc. https://www.inc.com/shelley-prevost/8-signs-youre-a-control-freak.html

Proctor, M. (2017, March 21). *6 science-backed ways being kind is good for your health - quiet revolution*. Quiet Revolution. https://www.quietrev.com/6-science-backed-ways-being-kind-is-good-for-your-health/

Psychology Today. (n.d.-c). *Flow*. Psychology Today. https://www.psychologytoday.com/intl/basics/flow

Psychology Today. (n.d.-d). *Optimism*. Psychology Today. https://www.psychologytoday.com/intl/basics/optimism#:~:text=To%20many%20psychologists%2C%20optimism%20reflects

Psychology Today. (2019b). *Learned helplessness*. Psychology Today. https://www.psychologytoday.com/us/basics/learned-helplessness

Reynolds, M. (2014, September 24). *How to use your intuition*. Psychology Today. https://www.psychologytoday.com/us/blog/wander-woman/201409/how-use-your-intuition

Ribeiro, M. (2019, July 4). What is compassion meditation? (+ mantras and scripts). Positive

Psychology. https://positivepsychology.com/compassion-meditation/

Riopel, L. (2019, November 28). *28 best meditation techniques for beginners to learn.* Positive Psychology. https://positivepsychology.com/meditation-techniques-beginners/

Rowland, M. (n.d.). *Kindness matters guide.* Mental Health. https://www.mentalhealth.org.uk/campaigns/mental-health-awareness-week/kindness-matters-guide#:~:text=Acts%20of%20kindness%20have%20the,in%20control%2C%20happiness%20and%20optimism.&text=They%20may%20also%20encourage%20others,to%20a%20more%20positive%20community

Schultz, J. (2020, July 24). *5 differences between mindfulness and meditation.* Positive Psychology. https://positivepsychology.com/differences-between-mindfulness-meditation/

Shero, P. (2019, January 3). *3 differences between optimism and positive thinking.* MasterMinds Leadership. https://mastermindsleadership.com/leadership-blog/3-differences-between-optimism-and-positive-thinking/#:~:text=Optimism%20makes%20an%20assumption%20about

Skills You Need. (2011). *Problem solving skills.* Skills You Need.

https://www.skillsyouneed.com/ips/problem-solving.html

Smoll, F. L. (2013). *Keys to effective goal setting*. Psychology Today. https://www.psychologytoday.com/us/blog/coaching-and-parenting-young-athletes/201311/keys-effective-goal-setting

Soots, L. (2016, September 22). *How I found laughter as a way to stay positive*. The Positive Psychology People. https://www.thepositivepsychologypeople.com/i-found-laughter-way-stay-positive/

Spencer, J. (2017, March 1). *How to pursue your life's calling*. Medium. https://medium.com/thrive-global/how-to-pursue-your-lifes-calling-29bf5f8a4f08

Stibich, M., & Gans, S. (2020, February 4). *Top 10 reasons to smile every day*. Verywell Mind. https://www.verywellmind.com/top-reasons-to-smile-every-day-2223755#:~:text=Smiling%20Makes%20Us%20Feel%20Good

Sutton, J. (2020, July 15). *The importance of mindfulness: 20+ reasons to practice mindfulness*. Positive Psychology. https://positivepsychology.com/importance-of-mindfulness/

Tartakovsky, M. (2012, January 30). *Signs of low self-esteem*. World of Psychology.

https://psychcentral.com/blog/signs-of-low-self-esteem/

Tartakovsky, M. (2017, October 16). *Coping with what you can't control*. Psych Central. https://psychcentral.com/blog/coping-with-what-you-cant-control/

Tynan, L. (2018, August 31). *Signs you're in a toxic work environment — and how to handle it*. Top Resume. https://www.topresume.com/career-advice/how-to-handle-toxic-work-environment

Ullén, F., de Manzano, Ö., Almeida, R., Magnusson, P. K. E., Pedersen, N. L., Nakamura, J., Csíkszentmihályi, M., & Madison, G. (2012). Proneness for psychological flow in everyday life: Associations with personality and intelligence. *Personality and Individual Differences*, 52(2), 167–172. https://doi.org/10.1016/j.paid.2011.10.003

Waley, M. (2019, November 7). *Ungrateful people: The "poison" of ingratitude*. Medium. https://medium.com/@murielwaleyxy/ungrateful-people-the-poison-of-ingratitude-16c69e917bbd

Whitaker, L. (2018, May 3). *How does thinking positive thoughts affect neuroplasticity?* MeTEOR Education. https://meteoreducation.com/how-does-thinking-positive-thoughts-affect-neuroplasticity/

Wilding, M. (2018, April 3). *3 simple steps to stop being a control freak.* Forbes. https://www.forbes.com/sites/melodywilding/2018/04/03/3-simple-steps-to-stop-being-a-control-freak/?sh=7c76083d6991

Wilner, J. (2013, July 7). *5 keys to accepting what you can't change.* You Have a Calling. https://youhaveacalling.com/emotional-health/5-keys-to-accepting-what-you-cant-change#:~:text=Acceptance%20has%20many%20benefits%3A

Wilson, M. (2011, February 25). *Creative visualization: The art of making negative thinking positive.* Under 30 CEO. https://www.under30ceo.com/creative-visualization-the-art-of-making-negative-thinking-positive/#:~:text=Creative%20visualization%20is%20the%20art

www.ingramcontent.com/pod-product-compliance
Lightning Source LLC
Chambersburg PA
CBHW020256030426
42336CB00010B/792